M000102182

Retire Rich
With Your 401(k) Plan:

A Complete Resource Guide with 100s of Hints, Tips, & Secrets from Experts Who Do It Every Day

By Heather Kleba

Retire Rich With Your 401(k) Plan: A Complete Resource Guide With 100s Of Hints, Tips, & Secrets From Experts Who Do It Every Day

Copyright © 2009 by Atlantic Publishing Group, Inc.
1405 SW 6th Ave. • Ocala, Florida 34471 • 800-814-1132 • 352-622-1875–Fax
Web site: www.atlantic-pub.com • E-mail: sales@atlantic-pub.com
SAN Number: 268-1250

No part of this publication may be reproduced, stored in a retrieval system, or transmitted in any form or by any means, electronic, mechanical, photocopying, recording, scanning, or otherwise, except as permitted under Section 107 or 108 of the 1976 United States Copyright Act, without the prior written permission of the Publisher. Requests to the Publisher for permission should be sent to Atlantic Publishing Group, Inc., 1405 SW 6th Ave., Ocala, Florida 34471.

ISBN-13: 978-1-60138-296-2   ISBN-10: 1-60138-296-0

Library of Congress Cataloging-in-Publication Data

Kleba, Heather, 1986-
  Retire rich with your 401k plan : a complete resource guide with 100s of hints, tips & secrets from experts who do it every day / by Heather Kleba.
       p. cm.
  Includes bibliographical references and index.
  ISBN-13: 978-1-60138-296-2 (alk. paper)
  ISBN-10: 1-60138-296-0 (alk. paper)
  1. 401(k) plans. 2. Retirement income--United States--Planning. I. Title.

  HD7105.45.U6K55 2009
  332.024'01450973--dc22
                          2009000935

LIMIT OF LIABILITY/DISCLAIMER OF WARRANTY: The publisher and the author make no representations or warranties with respect to the accuracy or completeness of the contents of this work and specifically disclaim all warranties, including without limitation warranties of fitness for a particular purpose. No warranty may be created or extended by sales or promotional materials. The advice and strategies contained herein may not be suitable for every situation. This work is sold with the understanding that the publisher is not engaged in rendering legal, accounting, or other professional services. If professional assistance is required, the services of a competent professional should be sought. Neither the publisher nor the author shall be liable for damages arising herefrom. The fact that an organization or Web site is referred to in this work as a citation and/or a potential source of further information does not mean that the author or the publisher endorses the information the organization or Web site may provide or recommendations it may make. Further, readers should be aware that Internet Web sites listed in this work may have changed or disappeared between when this work was written and when it is read.

All trademarks, trade names, or logos mentioned or used are the property of their respective owners and are used only to directly describe the products being provided. Every effort has been made to properly capitalize, punctuate, identify and attribute trademarks and trade names to their respective owners, including the use of ® and ™ wherever possible and practical. Atlantic Publishing Group, Inc. is not a partner, affiliate, or licensee with the holders of said trademarks. The "AARP" name and logo is a trademark and property of Retirement Made Simpler.

Printed in the United States
PROJECT MANAGER: Melissa Peterson • mpeterson@atlantic-pub.com
COVER DESIGN: Jackie Miller • sullmill@charter.net
INTERIOR DESIGN: Shannon Preston

 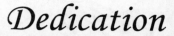# *Dedication*

This book was written for people who need a little help and encouragement setting up and investing their retirement accounts. Even if you are not a financial genius, you can retire rich and not have to struggle or worry about how to get by in retirement.

 # *Acknowledgements*

I would like to thank my wonderful husband-to-be, Mike, for always being there to give me support while working on this book and who always lent a proofing eye and encouragement when I needed it. Thanks to my mom and dad who have always been there to push me to try a little harder and give a little more, even when I thought I could not. Without your dedication to what I could be, I most likely would not be writing this book today. And to all of my family and friends, I am extremely thankful for your patience while I worked on this project — I know it took away from the time we spend together, and I am ready to make up for all of that now.

Table of Contents

Chapter 2: 401(k) Account Checklist   45

Chapter 3: People to Know, Things to Read   73

Chapter 12: Other Retirement Account Options   205

Chapter 13: 403(b) and 457 Plans   235

Chapter 14: Mistakes to Avoid and Questions to Ask   247

 *Foreword*

I was lucky. At an early age, my father started a savings account for me and sternly convinced me to save a part of my meager weekly paycheck. I was 12 and worked at a grocery store. I was truly fortunate to have that seed planted so early on. Sadly, most do not even think of saving until it is too late. Furthermore, our education system almost completely avoids the capital and credit markets and many high school graduates cannot even balance a checkbook.

The "world of finance" and Wall Street have set the stage for investing for the long term in their onslaught of tactics to market themselves and sell investing ideas to an unsuspecting and financially uneducated public. There is a huge emphasis put on diversification and how it will protect you for the long term. They have confused buy and hold with buy and hope. Commissions and fees are the fuel for most of their effort. I could go on and on about the misinformation that pours out of the financial institutions.

Corporate pension plans are being dumped, social security is in the tank, and our financial system is in the midst of a giant restructuring because the stability of the last 25 years has caused prudence, and what used to be called "common sense" is set aside for greater leverage and higher risk. Retirees are learning the hard way that "investing for the long term" has periods where the performance is poor and that those periods can last for most of one's retirement years. On June 30, 2008, the inflation-adjusted, total return on the S&P 500 for the last ten years turned negative. That means that those who retired in 1998 and put their hard-earned retirement money in a market index such as the S&P 500 — because it always goes up, right? — have not earned a penny in the last ten years. If they pay an annual fee for account maintenance, do not reinvest the dividends, or have a systematic withdrawal to live on, then they are truly hurting. Most retirement plans are set up with overly optimistic growth objectives based on very long term averages. Unfortunately, most do not have that long to recover and live on the hope that the market will take care of them. Hope is not a strategy. Also, I have yet to bring up the advances in medicine and pharmaceuticals that will cause people to live much longer than their retirement planning accounted for.

So, have I scared you yet? If I have, then that was my intention. If you have not yet begun to save for retirement, you need to start immediately, no matter what your age. Begin by reading and adhering to the advice in *Retire Rich With Your 401(k) Plan: A Complete Resource Guide with 100s of Hints, Tips, & Secrets from Experts Who Do It Every Day,* and you will have taken a great first step. Author Heather Kleba has covered all of the bases and done so with as much detail as one should need. The information provided in this book is extremely helpful. The tips and tricks that Kleba offers throughout are useful for anyone interested in learning more about retiring comfortably with their investments, whether an investment newcomer or a long-time investor.

Do not rely on the government to take care of you; take care of yourself. Reading this book is a great place to start. If you do not have the time or the inclination to actively manage your investments and, in particular, your retirement accounts, do not feel bad: Most people are in the same boat. Seek out an advisor who understands the important balance between safety and returns. To adequately grow a retirement account, one needs the type of growth provided by the equity market, but, unfortunately, you cannot afford the devastation caused by bear markets. My years of experience have taught me there are times when one should not be in the markets and are better off preserving their capital in cash equivalents because bear markets can set you back for very long periods of time. The closer to retirement you get, the worse the effect on your assets. It is critical that those managing your money understand the concept of avoiding the bad markets and trying to participate in the good markets. If they suggest holding stocks for the long run, then run from them.

Good luck in your investment endeavors and remember, it is never too early — or too late — to start saving for the future. Funding your 401(k) is the second step to get started in your planning for retirement. You have already taken the first by reading this book.

Gregory L. Morris

Big Canoe, GA

PMFM, Inc.

1061 Cliff Dawson Road

Watkinsville, GA 30677

800-222-7636

PMFM INC.
Personal Mutual Fund Management

# *Introduction*

Many of us do not know what we are going to do tomorrow, let alone 20, 30, or 40 years down the road. But your retirement is not as simple as choosing whether to go to the park or watch a movie — this is one of the most important stages of your life, and you need to plan accordingly. Many people will spend 20 to 30 years in retirement and will want to make the best of that time. You can start planning for your retirement by opening up a 401(k) or other retirement account. By doing so early, you can almost guarantee yourself a comfortable — if not lavish — retirement. Of course, if you are older and have not thought much about retirement planning, there is no time like the present. You can make up for lost time in multiple ways, and any retirement income is better than no income in retirement at all. You can live comfortably when you retire, as long as you form a solid plan and stick to it.

There are many reasons you need to plan for your retirement early and begin investing. One of the main reasons is that social security, even though it will ideally exist when you retire and provide you with a monthly check from the government, will never fully cover your day-to-day cost of living — not even the basics. Unless you have a pension plan that your company is required to offer, you need to begin planning for yourself. Even if social security and your pension plan are guaranteed, it is always nice to have extra money on which you can retire with a higher standard of living — it is easier to find $5 to save now than it will be to find $5 to pay for your basic needs in the future.

You would be hard-pressed today to find someone who thinks they do not need to worry about their retirement, but the amount of care you take in learning about how you invest is what differentiates one saver from the next; knowledge is proportional to yield. Think of a retirement account just like you would anything else in life — the more you know about it, the more successful you will be. Sure, there are exceptions to this rule, and you will see people making strange, impulse investments in their portfolio and coming out with tons of money, but this is the exception, not the rule. You do not need to be a financial scholar, but it is necessary that you know at least the basics of the 401(k) account you will own and the market into which you will be investing.

A well-planned retirement account can give you peace of mind when you leave the job force, knowing that you will have money coming in and that it will be enough to help you live not only comfortably, but rich if you follow some simple steps: sign up for your employer's 401(k) retirement plan, ask for any help you need, make wise investments, check in on your investments, update them when necessary, roll funds into one consolidated account when you retire or leave your job, do not rely too heavily on company stock, and formulate and follow a plan. While a retirement plan is not one-size-fits-all, you can use the basic rules and suggestions in this book to help formulate a solid retirement plan that best fits your needs.

This book was written for those who need information to make wise retirement account choices — be it what to invest in, how much to set aide, or whether it is smart to set up a second retirement account. We all want to retire comfortably — or even rich — and if that is what you are aiming for, then this book is for you.

What Is Up Next?

The following chapters will cover 401(k)s, common retirement issues, and many more topics in detail so that you can retire rich. Chapter 1 will give you a brief overview of the 401(k) plan and some of its quirks. Chapter 2 will discuss setting up your 401(k) plan, determining your eligibility, beneficiaries, and more. Chapter 3 will explain the different aspects of your plan, including whom to know and what documents you will need to pay attention to. Chapters 4, 5, and 6 will let you know about your different investment options and the risks and benefits associated with each one. Chapter 7 will cover taking risks to build wealth and maximize savings. Chapter 8 will let you know what you can do if you change employers after opening a 401(k) plan. Withdrawing funds will be covered in Chapter 9, and what to expect as you inch closer to retirement and finally retire will be covered in Chapter 10. Chapter 11 will help out those who need to save at any age, while Chapter 12 will reveal what to do if your employer does not offer a 401(k) plan or other retirement account options (Roth IRAs and more). Chapter 13 will explain 403(b) and 457 retirement plans. Chapter 14 will reveal mistakes that beginners and pros alike make, what you should avoid, and questions to ask throughout all stages of a retirement account. Case studies are scattered throughout the book and will give you insight into different investment companies and options. Finally, in the Appendix, you will find a glossary with important financial, tax, and 401(k) specific terms; Web sites to visit for more information; groups to contact if you need help; and other vital resources.

1   *The Basics of Retirement Plans*

In this chapter you will learn:

- What a retirement plan is

- What a 401(k) retirement account is

- What the retirement market looks like today

- What excuses people make from putting money away for retirement

- Why you should choose a 401(k) plan

Congratulations! By opening this book, you are on your way to financial freedom in retirement. But to be able to retire rich and kick back, there are some things you need to know and actions you need to take.

These days, saving for retirement is not difficult. Employers and the government have spent years trying to convince Americans that they need to save for their post-working years, and since it did not necessarily catch on as they had hoped, many employers have started doing the work for their employees with automatic enrollment plans and easy investment options. With things like this, it is almost difficult not to save for retirement. One-third of employers now offer automatic enrollment 401(k) plans, up from 19 percent in 2005, and 403(b) and 457 plans are following the same trend. According to Kiplinger, a personal finance and business forecasting company, half of the employers in the country offered automatic enrollment in 2008. A survey done by Retirement Made Simpler™ found that 95 percent of employees said the automatic plan makes saving easier, and 85 percent said they began saving earlier because of automatic enrollment. (Some investment experts, though, wonder whether automatic enrollment leads to complacency in retirement planning and investing.) In addition, thanks to a loosening of rules in 2006, employers are now able to assist their employees with investment advice through a third party.

Fast Fact

As of October 2007, the Employee Benefit Research Institute (EBRI) estimates that workers have invested $7.5 trillion in individual retirement accounts like 401(k)s.

Before you even consider retirement planning, you need to know about the upkeep of a retirement account. To start, be proactive in what you decide to do — this includes your investment strategy and the contributions you make to your account. Check in on your 401(k) account funds, look at your investments, decide if they have gone to the appropriate types, and check in on how those investments are doing. Make sure that your employer has appropriately set aside any matching funds for you, and find out when you will have full access to those funds. Also, write your retirement plan down, then check on it every once in a while. Did you have a baby? Get a divorce? Change jobs? You want your retirement outlook to reflect any change in your life that could affect you down the road. Finally — and this will be repeated throughout the book — be sure that you stick to whatever plan you create. While you can make adjustments as you see fit, do not decide to make early withdrawals or stop contributing to your account because the economy is not looking bright. You have to be in retirement planning for the long run, or at least long enough to formulate and see a plan through, or you will only hurt yourself.

Take a few moments to sit down and write out what you want or imagine your retirement to be like. Do you want to travel the world? Fulfill your lifelong dream of opening an antique store? Or just spend time at home with your grandchildren? How much will your retirement plans cost? What you want to do after leaving the workforce should help direct you as you make decisions regarding how much to set aside for your retirement account and how many chances you can take with your investments.

Fast Fact

According to the Employee Benefits Research Institute, only four out of ten workers have actually figured out how much they will need in retirement.

Action Item

Write down your retirement goals.

The Retirement Outlook Today

According to the 2008 Retirement Confidence Survey, a recent study of workers and retirees released by the EBRI, as the economy suffers, Americans are becoming increasingly worried about being able to retire and have enough money in retirement.

Fast Fact

According to Gregory Salsbury, in 2030, 32 states will have 17 percent of their population over age 65, much as Florida does today.

Only 18 percent of those surveyed said they thought they would have enough for a comfortable retirement, down 27 percent from 2007. In the survey's 18-year history, this is the steepest year-to-year decline.

Fast Fact

The Profit Sharing/401(k) Council of America says that 42 million workers are using their company-sponsored retirement plans, though, this number is decreasing.

Workers age 25 to 34 have the darkest outlook on retirement, along with those earning less than $35,000 per year.

According to a statement by Dallas Salisbury, president of EBRI, "The economy and health costs are major concerns," which contributes to people feeling like they cannot save for retirement.

The outlook seems equally grim for those who are already retired. Half of those EBRI surveyed said the cost of health care was higher than they had originally anticipated, and they now worry about whether they are still as financially secure as they once thought. One problem contributing to rising health care costs for retirees is the decline of employer-sponsored health care plans that stay with a person through retirement.

Fast Fact

According to the Employee Benefit Research Institute, in 2004, there were 52.2 million people contributing to defined contribution plans, down from 52.9 million in 2002.

Some experts see this decline as a blessing. If more current employees and soon-to-be retirees realize that they will have to cover health care costs in retirement, it may cause them to look more seriously at retirement planning. Right now, half of the workers EBRI surveyed have only $25,000 set aside for retirement. What is more astonishing is that 22 percent of workers surveyed and 28 percent of retirees included in the survey have no savings whatsoever. The study found that many people feel like they do not need to save much for retirement because they do not believe they will spend much during their non-working years. This may be true in some cases — transportation costs, dining out, work clothing, mortgages, and other spending will, or should be, reduced by the time you retire. Yet, increased health care costs and the potential need to pay for long-term care are fast becoming a drain for many retirees' savings plans. When asked to calculate retirement savings with a goal in mind, 59 percent of those surveyed increased the amount they were contributing to a retirement account or saving in another way.

Aging is not negotiable, and we cannot control it. What we can control is how we age and what we do when our working years have come to an end. This is best done with a 401(k) retirement savings account or other retirement account of your choice.

Another study conducted by an investment advisory company called Financial Engines Inc. found that, of approximately one million retirement portfolios they observed, more than two-thirds had unneeded risk, while about one-third held too much company stock. Though just about every investment advisor will recommend that you contribute enough to your 401(k) or other retirement account to be able to take full advantage of any matching funds your employer offers, one-third of those one million accounts were not following that advice. According to Jeff Maggioncalda, the CEO of Financial Engines Inc., in an interview with *The Dallas Morning News*, "The fundamental assumption that we made when we created the 401(k) is that people would do it themselves... And what we're realizing is that the fundamental assumption of a 401(k) is wrong. People are not doing a good job themselves." Those who are not high income earners are more likely to make poor investment decisions. Maggioncalda told the Dallas Morning News that he thinks we will no longer have 401(k) accounts that individuals will invest in themselves. He sees the country moving toward more automatic 401(k)s, in which employers will decide, at least initially, how much you contribute and where it is invested.

Does This Sound Like You?

There are many excuses for not taking the time to save for retirement. Some say that they do not have enough time in their schedule, but when you consider that two hours of planning could provide the finances they will need for 30 years, it makes sense to find the time. Others think that the state of the stock market should affect when they begin contributing to a 401(k) plan. They are afraid of buying shares when they are high. However, as you will read later, the fluctuations of the market, coupled with your consistent contributions to your plan, mean that sometimes you will buy high, but more often, you will buy low.

Not knowing much about the economy or how to invest is another common excuse, but the important thing to remember is that you do not need to be a financial genius to plan for your retirement — you just need to pay attention to a couple of tips, make a long-term plan, and stick with it. If your excuse is that you do not understand the 401(k) plan your employer offers, ask for help. You are better off feeling embarrassed and asking questions than having no money in retirement. There are many places you can go to for help, be they your own human resources division or one of the many companies that works to invest 401(k)s.

If you already had one bad experience with investing, try again. You are much more likely to do well the second time around, and you should never have pulled your money out of your retirement account or out of the market in the first place; bear in mind that there are no short-term fixes when it comes to investing in your future. Some people simply believe that they do not need to save for retirement and that someone else will be there to take care of them — "That is what I have kids for" or "The government will support me in retirement." Do not count on any of this. Your children will have their own lives and families to take care of, and the government is unlikely to come through with much in the way of money for retirement. Plus, for those of you who want to worry about today and not tomorrow — put the kids through college, pay the bills — think about your current lifestyle and decide whether you can accept living in poverty when you decide to leave the workforce or whether you want to stay in full-time employment for the rest of your life.

Fast Fact

According to National Public Radio, baby boomers will work longer than their parents and grandparents did.

The point is that there are no good excuses *not* to save for retirement. Your retirement years are supposed to be some of the best in your life, and you want to be prepared to spend them any way you please.

Retirement Plans

There are many different types of retirement plans available to you, and though this book focuses on the 401(k) retirement plan, you may be offered a different plan through your employer, or you may decide to go outside your employer and seek an additional retirement fund.

Defined contribution plans, like a 401(k) account, are considered — at this time — to be your best bet for having a secure retirement. You are not necessarily dependent on receiving money from someone else; this is all about you setting money aside for yourself. The 401(k) plan gives you the option to sign up through your employer and contribute pre-tax money to an account. If you choose to enroll in a 401(k) plan, it is possible that your employer will give you the opportunity to get matching funds, in which they will deposit a certain amount into your account based on your total contribution or your total annual salary. Another type of defined contribution plan is the 403(b) plan, which, unlike the 401(k), is offered to nonprofit organizations like schools or hospitals. The 457 plan is similar, and it is offered to public-sector (or government) employees. The contribution limits on the 457 plan are lower than most other defined contribution plans. There are also some universal savings plans in which you can take part, and these may be offered through your employer. Defined contribution plans are normally designed to be long-term savings plans.

A cash balance plan is another option when saving for retirement. These plans are similar to the defined contribution plans described previously. The cash balance plan, though, is actually a defined benefit plan, with the benefit considered to be a percent of what you earn at your job each year. When the money in these funds is invested, it is split up in a unique way. If your investment earns less than a 30-year U.S. Treasury bond, your employer will have to pay you the difference, but if your plan performs better than the 30-year Treasury bond, your employer is entitled to keep whatever is left over. The risk involved in a cash balance plan is taken on by your employer because he or she will be responsible for investing the money in your account. However, he or she normally has an incentive to do well, considering that he or she will get to keep any excess money. The cash balance plan is extremely portable.

Fast Fact

According to the Health and Retirement Study, the trend toward early retirement that many had planned or hoped for is being brought to an end partly by the decrease in defined benefit pension plans — workers now realize that they are on their own to save and that they need to save for a longer period of time. The Health and Retirement Study says that those with defined benefit plans retire about one year and four months earlier than those with defined contribution plans.

Fast Fact

According to the Retirement Security Project, the number of employers offering traditional defined benefit pension plans has declined by two-thirds over the past 20 years.

Pensions, defined benefit plans given to employees by their employers, are becoming less frequent. If you have a pension, you will receive a monthly check based on what you earned annually from your employer. Pension payments can be either fixed or adjusted for inflation and are heavily regulated by the government, right down to how they must be paid out to any account holders.

Fast Fact

According to the Employee Benefit Research Institute, only 37 percent of those in the workforce had a pension plan in 2005 and fewer employers were offering them to employees. Many pensions are ending up in the Pension Benefit Guarantee Corp., an underfunded government agency.

There is no right or wrong answer for each person's retirement plan: The most important thing to focus on is the fact that you are saving for retirement and are on your way to financial freedom when you hit the best years of your life.

Defined contribution plans and defined benefit plans are the two major types of retirement accounts that employers offer. Defined contribution plans include 401(k)s, SIMPLE 401(k)s, Safe Harbor 401(k)s, the SIMPLE-IRA plan, Employee Stock Ownership Plans (ESOPs), Employee Stock Purchase Plans (ESPP), and profit sharing plans. Cash balance plans offer a combination of benefits from defined benefit and defined contribution plans.

The differences between defined benefit plans and defined contribution plans are as follows:

1. Defined benefit plans are funded by the employer and, per federal law, employers must contribute a certain amount to ensure that the plan is funded enough for all employees. In a defined contribution plan, the employer can choose whether to make contributions (except in SIMPLE 401(k)s, Safe Harbor 401(k)s, money purchase plans, SIMPLE IRAs, and SEP plans). If an employer decides to make a contribution, it will come in the form of a matching contribution that could be a percentage of your pay or a certain amount based on what you contribute to the plan.

2. In a defined benefit plan, employees might not be able to contribute to the plan. In a defined contribution plan, the account does not exist until the employee makes a contribution (unless in an automatic enrollment plan, where the employee still makes a contribution but does not choose what that contribution will be at first).

3. In a defined benefit plan, the people in charge of facilitating the plan invest the money and make sure that the investments are enough to cover all of the employees in the plan. In a defined contribution plan, an employer chooses the types of investments available, but the employee is in charge of choosing where to invest his or her money among these choices.

4. In a defined benefit plan, the retirement benefit the employee receives is based on various factors, such as how many years that person has worked

for the company and their ending salary. In a defined contribution plan, the retirement benefit is based on what the employee contributed to the plan, what the employer contributed to the plan, and how the employee's investments performed.

5. In a defined benefit plan, retirees receive set annuity payments each month. In a defined contribution plan, there are many options for the retiree after retirement, including rolling the plan into an IRA, taking a lump-sum distribution, and purchasing an annuity.

6. In a defined benefit plan, the federal government guarantees that the employee will receive at least some benefits. The defined contribution plan has no federal guarantee, though there are some federal laws that must be followed that dictate how the plan is run.

7. In a defined benefit plan, if the employee leaves the current employer before retirement age, the money will stay with the employer until the employee tries to get it after retirement age is reached. In a defined contribution plan, the money in the account can be transferred to an IRA or another 401(k) plan or the employee can take the money out, though fees and taxes will apply.

8. In a defined benefit plan, the amount of benefits you have already earned cannot be reduced, but what you have the potential to earn in the future can be reduced. In a defined contribution plan, future contributions from your employer can be changed or stopped. Your employer can also choose to close the defined benefit or defined contribution

plan but cannot take away any benefits or any contributions you have already earned or made.

9. In a defined contribution plan, your contributions are always yours, and you cannot be denied them; that is, you are always vested in your own contributions. However it does take awhile to get your employer's matching funds, with the exception of the SIMPLE 401(k) and Safe Harbor 401(k), which immediately vests you in any employer-matching funds.

Action Item

A retirement plan needs to begin when your first job does.

What Is a 401(k) Anyway?

Fast Fact

According to the Profit Sharing/401k Council of America, 400,000 companies have 401(k) plans.

To start, let us discuss the basics. A 401(k) plan is a defined contribution, employer-sponsored retirement fund that allows any participants to contribute money from their salary in a tax-deferred fashion. As long as you sign up with your employer for the plan, money will be taken from your paycheck before taxed. That means that when the money is pulled from your paycheck, you receive a tax deduction because you will pay taxes on a lower amount, and you will not even miss the money. A 401(k) plan is especially helpful for the person who is not a good saver — you never see the money, so you have no chance to buy that new pair of shoes or make a down payment on that new car you have been eyeing.

The money will grow in your account tax-deferred, and you will only begin paying taxes on the earnings once you start withdrawing the money. But beware, this is only a federal tax break — some states and cities still require you to report the balance in your 401(k) plan and pay taxes on that amount each year.

Employers like to offer 401(k) plans for selfish and unselfish reasons. They like to get you in the door to work for their company by offering benefits such as 401(k) or other retirement savings plans. You should note that 401(k) plans are cheaper for employers than offering a pension plan because they are defined contribution plans, while pensions are defined benefit plans. Employers also like to help you — whether they feel obligated to or are looking to boost morale — be stable in retirement.

Fast Fact

According to the Employee Benefit Research Institute, the average balance in a 401(k) account in 2006 was $66,650.

A study conducted by John Shoven and David Wise at the National Bureau of Economic Research found that the tax-shelter features of 401(k)s that allow your account to grow tax-deferred could actually be a bad thing for some investors. Why? According to " A Guide to Managing Your 401(k)" published by *Newsweek*, any large withdrawals will require you to pay federal, state, and a 15 percent excise tax, meaning your tax rate can go up significantly. Anyone who inherits your 401(k) money upon your death can have their tax rate grow to 92 percent. So, once your 401(k) account is so large that it will trigger an excise tax if you make a withdrawal, you are better off saving your money outside of your current plan. For those retired with more than $1.2 million saved, be sure to withdraw all the money from your account, even if it means you will pay high taxes, because the taxes you pay today will be small compared to what your heirs would be required to pay.

CASE STUDY: ADVISOR COUNSELING AND PLAN APPROVAL

TIAA-CREF

1101 Pennsylvania Ave. NW,

Suite 800, Washington, D.C. 20004

www.tiaa-cref.org

jcompton@tiaa-cref.org

1-202-637-8938 – Voice

1-202-637-1260 – Fax

Daniel Keady, Director, Advisor Counseling and Plan Approval

One of the worst things someone can do in their investment strategy is select investments based on recent returns (chasing returns) rather than focusing on creating a diversified portfolio that matches their goals and risk tolerance. A proper overall asset allocation is the number one goal. Another mistake is failure to have a defined strategy to rebalance your portfolio when market swings have created over and under weights (e.g., stocks have grown for your target of 50 percent to 70 percent of your portfolio) back to your desired portfolio. Another mistake we see is people mistakenly focusing on "timing the market," or short-term buying and selling, rather than having a long-term perspective and staying with a properly planned overall asset allocation. People should instead plan to create a tailored income stream that will match their basic income needs, that is designed to keep pace with inflation, and that will provide flexibility to deal with unexpected expenses.

CASE STUDY: ADVISOR COUNSELING AND PLAN APPROVAL

A risky portfolio may subject an investor to extra risk for a given level of projected return. In essence, you are not getting paid for the risk you are taking. At a high level, diversification smooths returns and reduces risk because some asset classes may be going up while others are going down.

If you are new to investing, have a long-term perspective, and do not focus on day-to-day swings. Do not put all your contributions into low-risk investments, like money markets. You have to invest at least a little in growth assets, like equity funds.

If your investments have been hurt in the recent economic downturn, make sure that your overall asset allocation matches your risk tolerance. Remember that you are investing for the long term and that increased market volatility occurs from time to time. Your best strategy is to maintain a diversified portfolio based on your risk tolerance, have a long-term plan to reach your goals, and do not make emotional investment choices.

Young investors need an emergency fund. And in terms of retirement accounts, you need to save, even if the budget only allows a small amount, in a tax-deferred account to create a habit of saving and to take advantage of many decades of compounding your money. Starting early can, even with small sums, lead to very large sums, compared to waiting and trying to catch up by putting away larger sums in your late 40s. Moreover, it can be very hard to save enough for retirement if you wait until your 50s to start saving. As for older investors, they need to remember that retirement may last 30 years or longer, and one thing that will have an impact is the need to fund rapidly increasing post-retirement healthcare costs — these expenses will have a big impact over time, so plan for them now.

How Does a 401(k) Plan Work?

Briefly, a 401(k) plan works like this: You agree to let your employer take a specified amount of money from your paycheck each pay period to put into your retirement account. You, in turn, look at your different investment options and choose where you think your money will do best and invest a certain portion of your 401(k) balance. Each year, or more often if you wish, you will come back and look at your investments to see how they have been doing and reassess your situation to determine whether you should make any changes. Finally, you will retire with your 401(k) savings and, if you have planned carefully, live the life of luxury.

Why Should I Choose a 401(k) Plan?

Chances are, if you are just starting out, you think you will be better off just putting the money into a bank account. If you are a good saver, this is one option, but 401(k)s take the thinking out of saving. Another benefit of the 401(k) over a simple bank account is that many employers offer matching contributions to your plan (we will talk more about this in Chapter 2). But for now, all you need to know is that your employer is offering you free money — the bank does not do that. Another thing the bank will not do is invest your money into stocks or bonds where it has the potential to grow enormously. You will only receive a small interest payment — and the interest in a bank account is taxed by the government.

If you are still not convinced that the 401(k) plan is for you, you have two choices. Keep reading and find out how easy and manageable this type of retirement account can be, or cross your fingers that your social security checks will be enough to cover your basic needs after you retire.

Fast Fact

In 2001, Congress passed the Economic Growth and Tax Relief Reconciliation Act (EGTRRA), which is considered to be one of the most important tax law changes for retirement accounts. EGTRRA increased contribution and deduction limits for IRAs and employer-sponsored retirement plans and helped to make retirement accounts more portable from job to job. The actions set in motion by EGTRRA are set to expire in 2010, unless new laws are passed.

It Is Not All Rosy

Like all things in life, the 401(k) plan is not always rosy. You can make bad investment choices within your plan, the plan offered to you might not have decent investment options, or the economy can have a down year or two — all of this can affect your finances. The important thing is to know up front what your plan will do for you and what you need to do for your plan.

One of the most important things to pay attention to are the fees associated with your plan. Chapter 2 will discuss this in more depth, but bear in mind that while a 401(k) plan is better in the long run than a savings account, money is not as easy to withdraw, and there will be fees associated with any withdrawals made before age 59 and a half. However, some accounts will allow you to take loans out against yourself or make withdrawals for hardship financial reasons, but you should not count on or even plan on doing that. You will be penalized and end up hurting your final savings plan. Before age 59 and a half, you will be heavily taxed on withdrawals, owing the state, federal government, and localities taxes; there is also a 10 percent federal early-withdrawal penalty — some states impose additional penalties.

Some plans have additional fees built into them. In Chapter 2, we will look at this in more detail, but for right now, it is important to know that sometimes your employer will cover these fees and sometimes it is up to you. You may have to pay administrative fees, which could be a flat amount or a percentage of the balance in your 401(k) account, or investment fees, which are normally based on a percentage of the 401(k) plan you are investing into a specific stock or bond. You most likely will not even notice this fee because it is not directly charged to you, but rather comes out of the return on your investment; investment fees could be sales charges or management fees with an average of 3 to 4 percent. Some investors fail to realize that there are fees associated with investment accounts, and, according to Michael J. Fitzgerald, Masters of Tax Planning and Consulting President, this "is a one way ticket to nowhere."

401(k)s Are Not a Short-Term Fix

By and large, a 401(k) plan is not about how much you are investing (there are contribution limits), but about how long you invest for — see Chapter 11 for more information on what to do if you are nearing retirement and have not started saving yet. The reasoning behind this is that when you choose where to invest your 401(k) funds, you want to be in for the long-term so you can withstand the cyclical dips in the economy — essentially, if you are holding stocks, it means you are constantly buying more shares when they are at their lowest price and fewer at the highest price, which keeps your investments growing.

Is It Safe?

As you perhaps already know, any money you deposit in a bank (up to $100,000) is insured by the Federal Deposit Insurance Corporation (FDIC), meaning that if the bank goes out of business or someone robs the place, you will get your money back. While 401(k)s are not exactly the same, they are still a safe (and bountiful) place for investing your retirement funds. For private-sector employees (anyone not employed by the government), the Employee Retirement Income Security Act (ERISA) has minimum standards put in place by the government to protect you and your plan. Chapter 2 will explain exactly what this means, but for now, know that your plan is not insured by the federal government, but due to ERISA restrictions, if your employer should go out of business or take off with all the company profit, your 401(k) money will still be safe, and you will receive it when it comes due.

If you are a member of a union, and your plan is collectively bargained, ERISA protection rules may be different for you — see your summary plan description for more information. If you work for the federal, state, or local government, ERISA will not protect you.

Under ERISA rules, you can sue your plan fiduciaries to enforce your rights if: you have been denied a claim for benefits after taking part in the review process; you have benefits that have not yet been given to you that should have been; you have requested and plan documents but have not received them; the fiduciary breaches his or her responsibilities; or you want to stop the plan from doing something against ERISA rules. The Department of Labor will be the one to enforce ERISA rules.

A Little Something for Everyone

Whether you are choosing a 401(k) plan or another type of retirement account, it is important that you set up a savings plan that works for you. Think about your target retirement date and how much you will need to just get by, live comfortably, or live the high life. Kiplinger suggests that you assume you will need at least 80 percent of your current income to continue in your current life style during retirement. But, if you plan to retire rich, you will need to assume 100 to 120 percent of your current income. To calculate how much you will need in retirement, fill in the following worksheet, or visit these Web sites:

- **www.retirementcalc.com**

- **http://cgi.money.cnn.com/tools/ retirementplanner/retirementplanner.jsp**

- **http://moneycentral.msn.com/retire/ planner.aspx**

- **www.bloomberg.com/invest/ calculators/retire.html**

- **http://sites.stockpoint.com/aarp_rc/wm/ Retirement/Retirement.asp?act=LOGIN**

WORKSHEET: ESTIMATING RETIREMENT SPENDING		
Category	Current Spending	Anticipated Retirement Spending*
Food		
Housing		
Clothing		

WORKSHEET: ESTIMATING RETIREMENT SPENDING		
Category	Current Spending	Anticipated Retirement Spending*
Entertainment		
Travel		
Transportation		
Healthcare		
Education		
Other		

You should make these considerations based on your current age, what your retirement goals are, what other savings plans you already have in place, and what your current financial situation is, but do not count on your Social Security benefits to cover all your living expenses in retirement.

Taxes

This is an important place to discuss tax brackets so you can take a look at your taxable income and figure out what you will owe in taxes each year. By making good estimations, you will be able to put more away for retirement.

By law, the Internal Revenue Service must adjust tax brackets each year to account for inflation. In 2007, the federal government expanded the tax brackets for the 2008 tax year, meaning your tax rate may be lower than it was last year.

2008 TAX BRACKETS
SINGLE INCOME EARNERS

Taxable income at least...	But no higher than:	Tax:
$0	$8,025	10 percent of the amount over $0
$8,026	$32,550	$802.50 plus 15 percent of the amount over $8,025
$32,551	$78,850	$4,481.25 plus 25 percent of the amount over $32,550
$78,851	$164,550	$16,056.25 plus 28 percent of the amount over $78,850
$164,551	$357,700	$40,052.25 plus 33 percent of the amount over $164,550
$357,701	No limit	$103,791.75 plus 35 percent of the amount over $357,700

MARRIED COUPLES FILING JOINTLY

Taxable income at least...	But no higher than:	Tax:
$0	$16,050	10 percent of the amount over $0
$16,051	$65,100	$1,605 plus 15 percent of the amount over $16,050
$65,101	$131,450	$8,962.50 plus 25 percent of the amount over $65,100
$131,451	$200,300	$25,550 plus 28 percent of the amount over $131,450
$200,301	$357,700	$44,828 plus 33 percent of the amount over $200,300
$357,701	No limit	$96,770 plus 35 percent of the amount over $357,700

2008 TAX BRACKETS
MARRIED COUPLES FILING SEPARATELY

Taxable income at least...	But no higher than:	Tax:
$0	$8,025	10 percent of the amount over $0
$8,025	$32,550	$802.50 plus 15 percent of the amount over $8,025
$32,551	$65,725	$4,481.25 plus 25 percent of the amount over $32,550
$65,726	$100,150	$12,775 plus 28 percent of the amount over $65,725
$100,151	$178,850	$22,414 plus 33 percent of the amount over $100,150
$178,851	No limit	$48,385 plus 35 percent of the amount over $178,850

HEAD OF HOUSEHOLD

Taxable income at least...	But no higher than:	Tax:
$0	$11,450	10 percent of the amount over $0
$11,451	$43,650	$1,145 plus 15 percent of the amount over $11,450
$43,651	$112,650	$5,975 plus 25 percent of the amount over $43,650
$112,651	$182,400	$23,225 plus 28 percent of the amount over $112,650

HEAD OF HOUSEHOLD

Taxable income at least...	But no higher than:	Tax:
$182,401	$357,700	$42,755 plus 33 percent of the amount over $182,400
$357,701	No limit	$100,605 plus 35 percent of the amount over $357,700

* Many people are in higher tax brackets in retirement than while in the workforce because they have multiple forms of taxable income coming from pensions, retirement accounts, and social security, and most retirees are no longer making qualified plan contributions to retirement accounts — plan accordingly.

Things to Remember

Retirement planning is up to you, and even though many employers have initiated plans that automatically enroll you in a retirement account, you need to take action to ensure that your retirement funds are properly invested and taken care of. It is crucial that you pay attention to retirement, as it is one of the most important times of your life. There are multiple options for you in retirement plans, depending on what your employer offers, including defined contribution plans, cash balance plans, and pensions. Most importantly, a 401(k) plan is a good way to save because you are putting money into the account before you ever see it, meaning you have no way of touching it or spending it on something else.

Chapter 1 Summary

- Many workers have a grim outlook on retirement and believe they will not be able to save enough by the time they plan to leave the workforce.

- There is no good excuse not save for retirement.

- A 401(k) retirement account is a tax-deferred savings plan offered by your employer.

- A 401(k) account is not for short-term savings — you must be willing to invest for a long time; otherwise, you will not have good returns.

- While your 401(k) is not insured by the federal government, your employer is required to abide by rules and regulations, and you cannot lose your 401(k) money if your company goes bankrupt.

- 401(k) contributions come from your paycheck pre-tax, meaning that you will not be taxed on the amount you are contributing to the plan until you begin making withdrawals.

- 401(k)s are not free; there are fees associated with investing and account maintenance, which can range, on average, from 3.5 to 5 percent.

- A 401(k) plan offers you flexibility in deciding how you want to plan for retirement — you choose how much money to contribute to the account, how to invest it, and when to make withdrawals.

- 401(k) retirement plans are better than saving money in a bank account — the money in your 401(k) is much harder to access, it will grow much faster, and you do not have to make a conscious effort to save the money.

2
401(k)
Account Checklist

Taking that first step toward investing in your retirement can be daunting, but do not worry: We can do it together. If you are with a new employer or have just decided to sign up for your 401(k) plan, this chapter is for you.

In this chapter, you will learn:

- How to sign up for a retirement plan once you find out if you are eligible

- What fees are associated with a retirement plan

- How and why to choose a beneficiary

- What happens if the unexpected occurs

- How to find and pay hidden fees

Am I Eligible?

To begin, it is important to know that your employer is not required to offer a 401(k) plan, nor do they have to let all employees participate. If you are a union employee governed by a collective bargaining agreement, federal law prohibits giving you a retirement savings plan that has not been agreed to by your collective bargaining unit. Nonresident aliens can be excluded from the program, but those who live in the United States but are not citizens cannot be excluded — this category includes green card holders. Temporary employees can be excluded, as can those under 21 years of age as long as your employer excludes all persons under 21 — it cannot be on a person-by-person basis. Other groups of employees can be excluded from the plan as long as they make up less than 30 percent of the company's total employees.

After figuring out if you are eligible, you need to look into when you are eligible to begin contributing to the plan. Some employers have set up a plan that will allow interested employees to immediately begin contributing to their plan, while others make you wait until an "open enrollment" period comes up, which may come once per pay period or just once per year. It would be wise to find these things out during your interview, as you are better off at a job that offers a 401(k) plan that you can contribute to immediately. Be sure to ask about a potential employer's specific contribution schedule and what their timing descriptions are — for example, if they say one year, do they mean one calendar year or one anniversary year?

Be alert when you are a new employee — some employers put their employees into an automatic plan that signs them up once they are employees and begins pulling money from their paycheck. A plan like this may not be taking the amount out of your paycheck that you would like, and if you do not know you are involved in the program, you will not be able to invest your retirement plan the way you want.

If you are a part-time employee, you may be eligible to contribute to your company's 401(k) or other retirement plan as long as you work at least 1,000 hours per year (approximately 20 hours per week), but you need to check with the plan administrator or plan sponsor to see if this benefit is offered to you.

Fast Fact

While some employers require you to work one year before being eligible to contribute to the plan, others require more years of service if you are immediately vested in the plan.

Know Your Rights

If you are older, you cannot be denied participation in the plan because of your age.

Signing Up — The Basics

There are some terms you need to be aware of when signing up for your 401(k) plan. You can find all of them in the back of this book, but the first one to know about is the salary deferral form. You will need to fill out this form to enroll in the plan. The salary deferral form is essentially a statement of how much you plan to put into the account per pay period, which may be calculated in dollar amounts or percentages. If you are not salaried, and have an inconsistent pay amount, go with the percentages — it will make life easier for you and keep the amount of money coming in more consistent.

When deciding how much money to set aside, there are many things you need to consider. One thing to think about is how much you are allowed to contribute to your 401(k) account: per employer or per government rules. Each employer has a different set of rules on how much you can contribute to your account per year or pay period. One restriction is often placed on high income earners, at the bequest of the federal government, to ensure that the company executives are not designing a plan that is advantageous only to them. The government, on the other hand, has static rules based on your age. For those under 50, the maximum contribution in 2008 was $16,500 per year. But, once you turned 50, the government let you play catch-up and raised the maximum contribution an extra $5,500 to $20,500 in 2008. The federal government also imposes a percentage of pay limits, which will take into account any profit-sharing or 403(b) plans you participate in. One of the best ways to figure out exactly how much you will need in retirement is to use a retirement calculator. A list of multiple financial Web sites offering them can be found in Chapter 1.

Know Your Rights

Your contributions must be deposited as soon as possible into the 401(k) trust, but no later than the 15th business day of the month following your payday.

If you switch jobs during the calendar year, you are still required to abide by the contribution maximum. The $15,500 limit (or $20,500 limit, if you are 50 or older) applies to all 401(k) accounts, not to each separate one you have with each separate employer.

Action Item

Every little bit helps. Try to increase the amount you are contributing each time you get a pay raise or each time a major debt is paid off, such as credit cards, education, or your home.

You also need to think about how much you need to live on now and how much you can afford to invest. Think about how you want to retire — if you want a large nest egg, you will want to consider contributing more to the plan — as long as you can afford it. When considering how much you will need in retirement, it is important to remember that you will need less to get by then than you do now because by leaving a full-time job, you cut out many day-to-day expenses, like commuting, eating out, work clothes, and other current necessities. It is also commonly assumed that by the time you retire, you will have paid off your mortgage, assuming that you retire at or after age 60 and got a 30-year mortgage when you were in your 30s.

Fast Fact

According to Michael J. Fitzgerald, age should not be a factor in deciding when to retire. "Instead of focusing on time, focus on how to systematically replace 100 percent of your income adjusted for inflation. Then, you will not have to use the liquid asset classes to produce ordinary income. If you truly are a long-term investor, you should only use the equities market to outpace inflation and get your yearly pay raise for the markets, not pull out an inconsistent cash flow."

While it is important to begin investing right away, if you are unsure about how much you want to contribute, bear in mind that you can change the amount that is deducted from your paycheck each pay period or year

— simply contact your human resources department or whoever the contact is listed on your summary plan description and ask him or her to make a change. You may decide a few years down the road that you have more money available to put away for retirement or that you have been putting away too much. This is an important decision, but do not worry excessively about it now and waste too much valuable investment time.

Action Item

Save more than you think you will need — in the end, the worst that can happen is that you have money left over to give to your beneficiaries.

One of the most important things to think about is whether your employer offers any matching contributions. If they do, you will want to make sure you are taking advantage of the maximum they will give you — if they match up to 4 percent of your salary, then you will want to be sure to put at least 4 percent away; otherwise, you are missing out on free money. As mentioned in the beginning of this book, it is not always about how much you contribute but about how long you contribute for — sign up for your employer's 401(k) plan as soon as you are able to, even if you can only make a small contribution at first.

In thinking about what you can afford, you should note that even putting away the smallest amount, once compounded by interest and any matching contributions your employer offers (as long as you stick with the plan), will grow and benefit you in the end. You should strive to increase the amount you put into the plan each year.

Or, if you are unsure about your plan and want to adjust to having smaller paychecks, consider making small, consistent increases — like a certain percentage every six months or so.

Fast Fact

Occasionally, a blackout period may occur during which you will be unable to take out loans, receive distributions, or make investments for at least three business days — this generally happens when a plan administrator chooses to change investment options or record keepers; you are required to receive advance notice.

Action Item

When you plan for your retirement, have a goal in mind. This can include a decision about what you plan to do, but it should also include a decision about whether you will need your retirement account income to survive or whether you are simply planning to pass it on to your children, grandchildren, or whoever else might benefit from your plan.

* Take note that when you calculate your anticipated retirement spending, you will normally pay less for housing (considering your mortgage is paid off), clothing, food, and transportation expenses, but your health care costs will more than likely increase the older you get. On the other hand, some people find that they spend more in retirement because they take up new hobbies, travel, or enjoy more entertainment options, like movies, theater performances, or eating out.

Action Item

Consider your life, health, auto, homeowners, and other insurances to see whether it would be appropriate to increase or decrease what you are paying. This is a good time to figure out whether your employer will provide medical benefits in retirement or whether you need to apply for Medicare — do not see Medicare as a government handout — private insurance is expensive, even more so for those who are not working. But do not expect the government to pay for all your healthcare needs.

Retirement Myth

Fact or Myth?

I will have to spend more in retirement because of increased health care costs.

If you are worried about paying more for health care, you should figure this into your retirement savings. The truth is that your expenses will most likely go down: no more payroll tax, lower retirement account contributions, no new office clothes, and no going out to lunch. One study found that those who are over 75 spend about half as much as their middle-aged counterparts.

Variables

As with planning for any event, there will be unknown variables. When making a plan for retirement and deciding how much to contribute to your 401(k) account, you will need to think about any possible unknowns that may find their way into your life in the future. Some variables to consider include:

- Family emergencies

- Care for elderly parents

- Your own medical costs

- Any additional income you may have in retirement, including pensions and social security

- Any problems your children may have that require your help

- Inflation

- The return you will get on your investments

- Taxes

- How many years you will be in retirement and need your savings to last

Fast Fact

Especially if you have a long time before your retirement, remember inflation — this will influence how much you will need in the future (most people can expect to be paid more each year with a cost-of-living adjustment for inflation, but do not necessarily count on it): $1 million today will not go as far in 20 years.

The unfortunate part of variables is that you cannot plan for them. But, with repeated analysis and close attention to detail, you can make some educated guesses. You always want to make sure you have emergency money reserves, just in case the unexpected happens. You are better off putting more money away than you need and being extra padded in the future than having to scramble for a little extra cash if something happens. Diversification, discussed in more detail in Chapter 7, can help guard you against the unknowns of the economy, as can investing more conservatively as you grow older.

Automatic 401(k)s

An automatic enrollment 401(k) has a number of different features that makes it automatic. One is that employees are enrolled in the 401(k) plan automatically — unless they choose to opt out — which is a big difference from having no plan unless you opt in. The employee is still able to make a choice, but the automatic plan encourages people to save for retirement. There is also an automatic contribution where a specified percentage of pay is deferred into the plan — there is generally a set contribution at some level, and some companies offer automatic escalation, which means that every year an employee receives a pay raise, the automatic contribution taken from the employee's pay check will go up (typically this rise is about 1 percent). The theory is that this escalation is virtually painless on your wallet because you will never see that extra money in your paycheck. Another feature to the automatic enrollment plan is an automatic investment, which means an employee is automatically invested in a default plan. Before the Pension Protection Act, many employers used money market funds as the default, but now they are putting people into target date funds that shift over time based on the employee's target date for retirement.

An automatic 401(k) is like putting your retirement savings on cruise control. You do not really have to go back and look at your investments because they are automatically shifted, which is important because you will be protecting your nest egg as you get closer to retirement by moving into less risky investments, even though you are not as involved in the plan.

There are a number of plan administrators that offer automatic enrollment features, so an employer needs to speak with the company's current plan administrator to see whether this type of plan is offered or find a new plan administrator who does offer automatic enrollment. Sites like **www.retirementmadesimpler.org**, put together by the American Association of Retired People, Financial Industry Regulatory Authority, and the Retirement Security Project, help people understand what the benefits of an automatic 401(k) are for employers and employees, how employers can start offering one, and give employers a toolkit of information, including how to communicate about the new plan with employees.

The Financial Industry Regulatory Authority (FINRA) had 75 percent employee participation in its 401(k) plan before the automatic enrollment went into effect. Now, 97 percent of eligible employees participate. This is not unusual, according to FINRA, as most employers will see a 20 percent increase in participation.

The automatic enrollment program is helpful for many employees. Some take the theory of behavioral economics into consideration when looking at its strengths. People are comfortable with the status quo, and they do not want to make complex decisions. Saving for retirement can be complex when one needs to consider how much to contribute; how they can afford it; which investment funds to choose; and other various factors. Automatic enrollment helps with these decisions but always gives you a chance to change your mind.

Statistically, lower-paid workers and minorities benefit the most from an automatic enrollment plan because these groups of people are least likely to participate in other retirement account options. No one is disadvantaged by this plan because it offers employees the option to leave the plan if they are uncomfortable or cannot afford to be in it.

Nationally, larger employers were the earliest adopters of the automatic enrollment 401(k) plan, but now, an increasing number of employers have started to look into and begin this program. Most helpful in spreading the word has been education plans that lay out the basic facts for employers and provide them with the research and information they need to make their decision easier. Of course, this plan is not perfect for every employer, but based on statistics, most employers should consider it. In a FINRA study, when employees were asked what they thought about automatic 401(k)s, 98 percent were glad the plan was offered, 97 percent agreed that it made saving easier, and 85 percent said it helped them to save earlier than they would have without it.

Automatic enrollment 401(k) plans are particularly useful right now, not only because saving for retirement is important at any point, but because it is important to teach younger employees the benefit of saving early when they might not be considering it. It is a challenge to get young employees to save because they do not see themselves in retirement. FINRA runs many seminars on retirement and retirement savings, and according to them, the people who show up most often are not in their 20s or 30s, but are in their 40s, 50s, and 60s — ages when most people begin to focus on retirement. What younger investors need to know is that it is less painful to save when you are younger because you do not have to play catch-up and contribute large sums. Besides, once you are older, you may find yourself paying for elderly parents or a child's education.

If an employee decides to opt out of the automatic 401(k) plan within a certain period, the contributions already made are given back to the employee through the payroll system. But you only have a set time to leave the plan, and if you go past that deadline, you cannot just begin taking money out of the plan. You will either need to take a hardship withdrawal or loan, change jobs and roll it over, take a lump sum and pay the penalties, or just wait until retirement to take it out. The biggest problem with changing employers is that many people choose to just withdraw the money from the 401(k) account instead of rolling it over; this drains their savings.

Automatic enrollment 401(k)s have been proven to work. The Web site **www.RetirementMadeSimpler.org** features a number of success stories. When the automatic plan was instituted at FINRA, only a few employees chose to opt out of the plan — mostly because they could not afford to contribute at that time.

It is important for employees to remember that even though your employer is taking care of the enrollment and investment, you cannot be lazy about retirement. Look at how much is being taken out of your account and where it is being invested. If you are not happy with either feature, change it to make it fit your lifestyle and your plans for retirement. At least once per year, you must be offered the opportunity to change the amount being withdrawn from your paycheck or leave the plan entirely.

> ### Fast Fact
>
> When Congress passed the Pension Protection Act in 2006, many employers saw this as an opportunity to automatically enroll employees in retirement plans to encourage more saving. One of the greatest, and largest, success stories here was at Nationwide Financial Services, where more than 90 percent of employees participate in the company's retirement plan. According to the *Washington Post*, two years ago only 74 percent of employees were saving for retirement — now that number is up to 96 percent. In this type of plan, typically 3 percent of wages is taken from an employee's paycheck pre-tax and put into the retirement account — the employee does have the chance to opt out.

> ### Fast Fact
>
> States are considering offering automatic enrollment for government employee 457 plans. Alaska was the first state to implement automatic enrollment but only because its defined benefit plan was no longer open for any new hires. The tough thing about offering something like this in the public sector is that the state legislature must make an exemption for the plan — otherwise, it can be seen as garnishing wages and could raise multiple legal issues.

Pre-tax as Opposed to After-tax Contributions

Most 401(k) accounts have you contribute only pre-tax money, but some allow you to contribute after-tax money (the money left in your paycheck after taxes have been taken out) as well. There are benefits and drawbacks to making an after-tax contribution. One downside is that you will not see a tax benefit now because you will still be paying taxes on the same amount of salary, but you will get to keep your contributions in a tax-deferred account. Most employers will not contribute matching funds to any contributions made after-tax, but be sure to check with your employer when you sign up for your plan. Making an after-tax contribution is beneficial for those who cannot contribute the maximum amount allowed under federal or employer rules because they are considered highly compensated, but would rather continue contributing to a 401(k) plan than open up an Individual Retirement Account (IRA) or annuity (discussed in detail in Chapters 12 and 6). It is necessary that you always contribute the maximum allowed in pre-tax contributions before even thinking about making an after-tax contribution to your 401(k) account. By not following this rule, you will miss out on the tax benefits. The good news about after-tax contributions is that you cannot be double taxed on them — meaning that when you decide to make a withdrawal, you will not be taxed on what you take out of the account.

Who Does Not Want Free Money from Their Employer?

Many employers offer matching contributions to 401(k) plans to encourage their employees to plan and save for the future. Yet, as with everything else, there is a catch; this catch is known as "vesting." Any money you contribute to your 401(k) plan is yours, but anything your employer contributes to your plan may not immediately be yours.

Full vesting periods vary from employer to employer. This is another area where it is important to pay attention to timing — the amount of time your employer requires for their money to be completely vested begins when you become an employee of the company, not when you open your 401(k) plan. The federal government requires companies that do not immediately consider their contribution yours to follow one of two vesting rules — gradual vesting over seven years or less (with a specific percentage being vested each year) or immediate vesting after five years or less.

There are two types of vesting — cliff and graded. Cliff vesting is meant to help those who move from job to job frequently, such as women who sometimes have to leave the workforce to care for their family. In this type of vesting, you will own none of the matching funds until you reach a certain year of employment with the company — this is less common in 401(k) plans and more common in defined benefit plans. Graded vesting means that any matching funds your employer contributes are yours in increasing portions — for example, in four-year grading, you may receive 25 percent of your employer's contribution each year. Once you are fully vested, you cannot be denied those employer contributions.

If, for some reason, you leave your employer and come back to the same employer, you may be able to count these years of absence toward your vesting schedule, unless your absence was five years or equal to the number of years you previously worked for this employer — whichever is greater. Check with your plan sponsor to see whether this is allowed in your plan.

Some employers choose to offer a profit-sharing program rather than matching contributions. This is known as a non-matching employee contribution. In this case, you will receive an amount determined by your salary and the amount the company made that year; some companies may decide not to hand out any profit-sharing funds if they are having a bad year. Most often, you do not even need to make contributions to any sort of retirement plan to receive profit-sharing funds. A non-matching contribution may also be offered, not based on profits, but on an amount equal to a certain percentage of your pay for that year.

Carefully read all the documents given to you by your employer to determine what types of pay will be considered for matching funds. For example, you will want to find out whether overtime and tips count when your employer considers any matching funds, or if only your base pay will be taken into account. Your summary plan description is the best place to look for this (see Chapter 3 for more information on the summary plan description).

Beneficiaries

Unless you plan to never die, you must name a beneficiary; it is also a good idea to name a secondary beneficiary. If you do not fill out the beneficiary designation form with your 401(k) enrollment package or keep it updated to ensure your beneficiary is still living, the money in your 401(k) account at the time of your death will not go to the person you intend. Contrary to popular belief, you cannot control how your 401(k) money is distributed through your will.

If you are married, it does not matter who you have listed as your beneficiary when you die. Your spouse will automatically receive the money, unless he or she signs a waiver.

It is wise to have primary and secondary beneficiaries. Then, in the event of your death, the money will be directed to the person on that list who is first in line and still alive. You can also allocate a percentage of your 401(k) funds to each beneficiary to ensure they all receive some benefit.

If you have young children and want the money to go to them, it is wise to set up a trust fund and have the money from your account sent straight there upon your death. That way, you are not giving money to children who may be too young to handle it or do what is best for their futures with it.

Find out how your beneficiary will receive your 401(k) funds in the event of your death. Also, look into how your beneficiaries and the money in your account will be taxed. It will likely be subject to income tax and the federal estate tax, if you qualify.

Money left to your beneficiaries does not necessarily rollover to an IRA or Roth IRA. Your beneficiaries can covert the money to an IRA or withdraw the money from the account all at once. Of course, if they choose the latter option, they must pay a tax, but the money will not be subject to an early withdrawal penalty.

Talk to your beneficiary about your plan. He or she will be in charge of making many important decisions about it in the event of your death. Be especially sure to explain how withdrawals can be made when you die.

There Is No Such Thing as a Free Lunch

There are fees associated with having a 401(k) plan. Fees can be categorized as administrative, investment, or management fees. There are many ways you can find out about fees that will be charged to you. If you invest in bonds, the prospectus document you will receive once per year will include a listing of the fees charged to you, except for wrap fees. Wrap fees are charged to you for bundled services such as research and advice offered by a broker. Your account statement may also list your fees, as will your summary plan description, or annual report of your plan. But beware, many of these documents may not list your fees as such — the fees may be hidden in the plan. Some fees are not listed in dollars, but rather in "basis points," where 100 points is equal to 1 percent of the money you have invested.

Administrative fees are chiefly for record keeping. This fee might be paid by you or your employer, so you may not even realize that this fee exists, or it may be categorized as an investment fee. Administrative fees are paid as a flat rate or as a percentage of the money in your account.

Investment fees are related to what you invest in and are normally a percentage of your investment. These fees can be different, depending on whether you invest in an actively managed or passively managed fund. Passive funds are otherwise known as index funds. Your fund manager will invest money in stock indexes. This leads to lower fees because the mangers do not make many decisions or spend that much time making changes. Active management means the investments are watched over by a fund manager who constantly makes changes to help the performance of the fund. He or she will invest in stocks rather than indexes. The goal of the active manager is to beat the index fund return by 1.5 to 2 percent, which can often be difficult.

Investment fees will not be charged directly to you; they will instead be deducted from the return on your investment. Investment fees pay your fund manager, as long as you are involved in an actively managed fund. Sometimes, you will encounter a sales charge. This is what a mutual fund will charge as you buy and sell shares with your 401(k) plan money. There are a few terms involved with the sales charge.

- Front loading: A fee charged when you buy shares (based on your initial investment)

- Back loading: Fees charged when you sell shares

- No-load fees: Annual 12b-1 fees

Another type of fee you may encounter is the management fee. This is a basic maintenance fee based on the percentage of your money you have invested in a certain place. These fees are often charged on "benefit transactions," meaning that if your plan offers extra services, such as loans or hardship withdrawals, you will pay a fee on each transaction.

No matter what your plan manager tells you, no plan is ever run for free. Be wary of anyone who tells you there are no costs involved, and keep an eye out for hidden costs. If you are paying more than 1 percent of your balance in fees, it is likely too much. But do not forget to consider why your fees are so high. If your investment offers numerous bells and whistles, and if that is something you are looking for, then the higher fees may be justified.

A Tip from ShareBuilder

Employers: If you are considering a 401(k) plan for your business, look under the hood and ask about participant fees. Be wary of the hidden fees and high-expense fund offerings of some providers. We believe "all-in" participant fees should be 1 percent or less (this includes fund expense ratios, asset management fees, and wrap fees) so your money can work harder for you over time, which is why we believe in 100 percent transparent pricing.

To try to figure out what your fees are, look at the expense ratio for each fund you own (check **www.kiplinger.com/tools/fundfinder** or your own 401(k) account Web site), then multiply this number by the ending balance in each fund.

Fast Fact

Smaller companies have more fees because the company cannot afford to pick up all the fees and/or needs a special broker to coordinate the plan, who may charge higher fees.

Action Item

Talk with your employer if you think your fees are too high — ask him for other investment options.

You Are Not Insured

As noted in the introduction, the money in your 401(k) account is not insured by the federal government. Because of this, if you are seeking the utmost of safety and security, it is best to put your money into a FDIC-insured bank account. But, if you plan to make any money for retirement, the 401(k) is your best option.

While there is no direct federal guarantee on your money, the feds have taken some steps to make sure you will not lose your initial investment. This is known as the Employee Retirement Income Security Act (ERISA). This federal law governs how 401(k) plans work. Be careful — ERISA only governs private-sector companies.

One of the stipulations says that your 401(k) money cannot be mixed with your company's other assets, and that only the plan holder (you) can access the funds. Your employer must also:

- Regularly provide you with information on your plan, including but not limited to, the summary plan description

- Tell you how long before you are fully vested (if your employer offers matching contributions) and how long before you can participate in the 401(k) plan

- Let you know about the plan fiduciary so you are able to sue if he or she breaks rules laid out by your employer

- Allow you to make frequent changes to your investments

Only your employer or another plan fiduciary can be held legally responsible for your initial investment. You, as the plan holder, are responsible for choosing investments and, therefore, you are responsible for your plan's performance. But, you do not need to worry if your employer goes out of business, as your money is not gone, because the 401(k) plan money is held in a trust separate from business expenses. There is no legal claim to these funds (even by the federal government in the case of company or personal bankruptcy) by anyone other than you or your beneficiaries (in case you die before the company goes under).

Your employer must also follow 404(c) laws governing 401(k) investment plans, meaning he or she must:

- Offer three or more different options for where you can invest your money (stocks, bonds, or mutual funds, for example), some of which must be with high risk, some with low risk, and some offering medium risk

- Give you the information necessary to make decisions regarding your investments

- Give you the option to reinvest your money every three months or less

What Will Happen to My Money If...

I declare bankruptcy
If you declare bankruptcy, your 401(k) funds will be protected. Federal law prohibits creditors from forcing

you to take money from your retirement account to pay your debts.

I get a divorce

If you get divorced, your spouse or other dependent can claim a portion of your benefits as payment for alimony, child support, or any other necessary bills. The court can issue a Qualified Domestic Relations Order (QDRO), which will require this payment to be made. Your spouse can also choose to leave the money in the plan until a later date if the court order allows it. If he or she chooses to withdraw the money, he or she will not have to pay the 10 percent early withdrawal penalty but will have to pay any necessary income taxes on the amount withdrawn.

I die

When you die, your beneficiary (normally considered to be your spouse, if you have one) can choose to withdraw the money in a lump sum or roll it into a special IRA. Whether he or she chooses to make the lump-sum withdrawal or roll the money into an IRA, there is no 10 percent early withdrawal penalty that needs to be paid, but, as with a divorce, necessary income taxes must be paid on the amount withdrawn, and if you qualify, estate taxes will also be charged on the amount taken out of the retirement account.

My employer goes bankrupt or improperly handles my account dollars

If your company goes out of business because of fraud or some other form of corruption, your retirement funds may be at risk, but you should be able to recoup at least some of the money, because your employer is required to purchase a fidelity bond before setting up a 401(k) plan for employees, which helps to ensure that you receive at least some of your money back in this case.

However, if the company you work for goes out of business before your payroll contribution to your retirement account makes it into the trust, you may lose that chunk of money.

If your plan is closed, you immediately become 100 percent vested in any benefits you have earned, even if you were not yet fully vested. If the plan is only partially terminated, only affected employees will be immediately 100 percent vested in the plan. If your company is merged, and your plan is cut, the benefits you have already earned cannot be reduced. In any of these cases, plan fiduciaries must maintain the plan until all the due benefits have been paid.

If a company goes bankrupt, merges with another company, or acquires other companies, it can result in the employer leaving their current employee investment plans, meaning there is no fiduciary to manage your money. This can be difficult for employees when they want to get to their benefits or ask simple questions. The Department of Labor has responded to this problem by creating a voluntary process for the account custodian to keep the account open until all benefits have been paid out and the plan can be properly closed.

Worst-Case Scenario

One scenario that has not yet left the minds of those with retirement accounts deals with the collapse of Enron. When the company collapsed in 2001, there were approximately 2,000 companies offering retirement plans that were full of company stock, according to the Employee Benefits Research Institute — either by the employee's choosing or because the employer offered matching contributions only in the form of company stock. Enron employees were holding onto more than $1 billion in company stock. This raised the question of whether there should be a limit on the amount of company stock you can offer or your employees can purchase. A study conducted at that time found that out of 219 large companies with retirement plans, 25 had company stock that made up at least 60 percent of the assets.

Chapter 2 Summary

- Check with your employer to find out if and when you are eligible to contribute to a 401(k) account.

- Do not let the fees put you off from making contributions to your 401(k) plan or investing the money, but make sure the fees you are being charged are not too high.

- Be sure to choose your beneficiaries wisely and update them whenever you have a change in your life — divorce, death, or birth, just to name a few. Keep your beneficiaries well informed of how they will receive your 401(k) funds in the event of your death.

- If you declare bankruptcy, your 401(k) money cannot be taken from you.

- If you get divorced, the court can order you to give part of your 401(k) account funds to your spouse.

- Your employer may offer matching contributions for any contribution you make to your 401(k) plan. If he or she does, be certain to contribute enough to your 401(k) account to ensure that you are receiving the maximum matching funds from your employer.

- Your 401(k) contributions will normally be taken from your paycheck pre-tax, but some plans allow you to make contributions after tax as well. Before making any after-tax contributions, be sure you are making the maximum pre-tax contributions. You may not receive matching contributions from your employer for after-tax money.

- As of 2008, you can contribute a maximum of $16,500 to your 401(k) account per year. If you are over 50, the government lets you play catch-up, and you can contribute an extra $5,500 per year for a total maximum of $20,500.

- Begin making contributions to your 401(k) account as soon as you are eligible. Even the littlest bit helps.

- Deciding how much you will need when you retire and how much to contribute to your 401(k) account can be difficult. There are many variables to take into consideration, but if you sit down, make a solid plan, and stick with it, you can retire comfortably or better.

- If you do not abide by the contribution maximums, you will be penalized.

- There are unknowns — we must make educated guesses about them when planning how much we will need and how much we need to put away for retirement.

3 People to Know, Things to Read

In this chapter, you will learn:

- What documents you will receive and why they are important

- Who's who in your plan and why you need to know them

- What to do if you need help

So now that you have opened your plan, what happens next? Your employer will give you many important documents that explain your plan in detail — hang on to these and any new documents you are given. If you do not receive the documents detailed in this chapter, ask your employer or plan sponsor for them. Be sure to read everything you receive — both when you sign up for your plan and as you progress and receive quarterly or annual information. If you do not understand some of the information you have been given, or if you feel like you need more information, do not hesitate to contact your plan sponsor or administrator and ask for clarification. It does you no good to understand 401(k) plans broadly but not understand your own plan specifically. Plus, just because your withdrawals looked correct on your first pay stub after enrolling, do not assume they will always be right. Check each pay stub you receive to ensure the correct amount is being withheld for your retirement account.

Fast Fact

In your 401(k) plan, fiduciaries include the trustee, investment manager, and plan administrator.

Any fiduciary is required to act only in the interest of those participating in the plan and to help them maximize results for retirement benefits. Any duty taken on by a fiduciary must be done skillfully, follow any documents in your plan, properly diversify investments, avoid any conflict of interest, provide you with any necessary information to further your understanding of the plan, and pay any reasonable fees not passed on to you. If your fiduciary fails to behave in the manner required, they become liable for money lost because of whatever they did. For example, if your employer is not sending your 401(k) contributions to the plan but is rather holding on to them as company assets, they need to give you those contributions back, as well as any earnings you would have made in the plan.

A few notes for employers: You, too, need to review your plan from time to time. Many employers feel like they do not have problems, do not have time or money to look into the plan, would not know how to fix a problem, think a financial audit will cover any issues, or do not want to bring any problems to light. But just as a retiree must look in on his or her own assets to ensure that they are performing properly, so must an employer. If there is a problem, and it is allowed to continue, there is no telling how much damage you could do to your employees. If you catch problems early, you can fix them with less trouble and less money. During the past 25 years, there have been 10 major changes to pension law, and that means that if you have not looked in on your plan in quite some time, there is a good chance that many regulations may be different.

A mistake is not going to correct itself. The IRS should not be seen as a bad thing when there is a problem with your plan — they are there to help your employees more than they are there to hurt you, and many problems can be corrected without the IRS getting too involved.

However, just like a retiree, do not check in more often than necessary. You need to choose and keep a long-term plan so that your employees will have something they can stick with and rely on.

Important Documents

When you sign up for your 401(k) plan, you will receive many documents, and they will continue coming to you throughout your time in the plan. These documents will cover the basic details of your plan, how much you have in your account, what investments you have, what kinds of fees you are paying on your 401(k) account, and more. Not reading the material can lead to costly mistakes. Be sure to read and understand everything you are given.

The Summary Plan Description (or a document similar in name) will be given to you when you enroll in your 401(k) plan. This document will include details on your employer's plan and will be presented in easy-to-understand language. You should expect to receive an updated document every five years. Each time you receive an update, be sure to read and understand it. It will help you to understand matching funds, vesting rules, your eligibility, beneficiaries, withdrawals from your plan, and your legal rights. Furthermore, it will tell you who the plan administrator and trustee are and how you can reach them should you have any questions or concerns.

You will also receive a plan statement about your account. This must be distributed to you at least once per year, but many plans distribute it quarterly. The plan statement will let you know how your plan is doing, where your money is invested, whether you have accrued any interest, and whether you have made any withdrawals. Sometimes, this document will include information on your rate of return. The statement is not, however, required to explain or list the fees you pay on your account.

If you invest in mutual funds, you will receive a prospectus. This document will include information on your investment managers and what stocks or bonds your plan invests in. It may also include information on how each of the investments works and how well each one has performed over time. How often your fund manager buys or sells shares may also be included, as will fees, though the wrap fees will not be listed.

If you need to request additional copies of any necessary plan documents, you may be charged a copy fee. There are some documents you may want to have but will not receive up front, including the plan's Form 5500 annual financial report and the written plan document (check your employer's Web site for this information). You can also receive Form 5500 from the U.S. Department of Labor, EBSA Public Disclosure Facility, Room N-5638, 200 Constitution Ave., NW, Washington, D.C. 20210, or by calling 202-693-8673. Should your employer refuse to supply you with any particular documents, even if you pay necessary fees, the Employee Benefits Security Administration is a good place to contact.

Whenever you receive a statement of the benefits offered to you by the plan you are signed up for, check to ensure that your name, address, salary, contribution amounts from you and your employer, years of service, social security number, beneficiaries, marital status, investment performance, and fees are all correct.

When should you expect to receive important documents?

- Summary Plan Description: Before you reach the three-month mark of being involved in the plan. You must receive an updated copy every ten years — every five years if significant changes are made.

- If any changes to the plan are made, you will receive the summary of material modifications up to seven months after the end of the plan year.

- The Summary Annual Report will have information about your plan that shows up on the Form 5500 your employer files with the IRS — you will receive this either two months after the report filing deadline or nine months after the end of the plan year.

- A Notice of Significant Reduction in Future Benefit Accruals will only make its way to you if a significant change will affect what you will receive through your 401(k) account in the future. You will receive this as soon as your employer is able to put it together, within a reasonable time before the changes go into effect.

- The blackout notice will come your way if you will be unable to take loans, distributions, or change your allocations for more than three consecutive business days. You must receive this document no less than 30 days before the blackout is set to take place.

- Notice to Participants of an Underfunded Plan: For those in a defined benefit plan, if your plan dips below being 90 percent funded, you will receive a report two months after the report filing deadline.

- Individual Benefit Statement: You can receive this if you apply for it in writing from your plan administrator — you can receive this document as many times as you wish, but you will only be able to receive it for free once a year.

Who to Know in Your Plan

There are many people you need to be aware of who aid in maintaining your 401(k) account. Each of these people should be listed in your summary plan description, along with their contact information. These are the people you will go to with questions or for any sort of assistance with your plan.

Plan Sponsor

Your plan sponsor is your employer. He or she will make many different decisions about your plan, including where you are able to invest your 401(k) account dollars. Your plan sponsor has fiduciary responsibility, meaning that anyone with a decision-making role in your 401(k) plan's investments is legally bound to make those decisions in the best interests of the plan participants (you and your coworkers) and not in the best interest of the company, the plan provider, or anyone else.

CASE STUDY: CHUCK SNYDER, VICE PRESIDENT

Summit Plastic Co.
P.O. Box 117, Tallmadge, OH 44278
www.summitplastic.com
info@summitplastic.com
330-663-3688 — Voice
330-663-9738 — Fax
Chuck Snyder, Vice President

The president of the company and I are plan sponsors. I handle most major human resources decision-making within the 401(k) plan. In this role, we take the responsibility that we are offering a competitive product to our employees and that everything is happening in a legal, ethical manner. Annually, we analyze the performance of our plan's funds with the national averages for similar funds to ensure that we are in line with the industry trends.

As an employer, we cannot and do not give advice on funds or market performance. We do, however, try to help our employees understand the value of preparing for their futures. We believe it is in their best interests to participate, given our company match ($.25/$1.00 up to 6 percent) and the longstanding positive performance of our funds and 401(k) plans in general. We also have our financial advisors from Merrill Lynch visit us frequently to educate our employees and answer questions. In addition to education sessions, every employee gets a packet of

CASE STUDY: CHUCK SNYDER, VICE PRESIDENT

information from our plan administrator (Paychex) detailing the fund options, fund performances, and participation procedures. We offer open enrollment sessions with enrollment information twice annually.

Just prior to every open enrollment period, newly eligible employees (one year service) will receive a package from our plan administrator detailing the funds and sign-up procedure. We also attach a letter from HR detailing our match, vesting, and other features. Upon termination, an employee receives a package from the plan administrator detailing their rollover options.

In terms of our available investments, we have selected a group of funds offered by Merrill Lynch. We have options to change, add, or remove funds offered, and this has happened. We have also investigated funds recommended to us by employees. However, the performance of our funds has been good, and we have not seen the need to make large-scale changes, except for the addition of a few new funds in 2006. I have been working with the 401(k) plan for more than 15 years. In that time, I have unfortunately seen a decrease in the number of participants in our plan. It appears the tight economy puts pressure on addressing immediate financial needs versus saving for the future.

Action Item

If you have problems, contact the plan sponsor or plan administrator and ensure that a correction is made — do not let it go unnoticed or unfixed.

Plan Trustee

The plan trustee is someone who acts instead of your employer to upkeep and monitor your 401(k) account. The trustee will normally be a bank or investment company. This person takes over fiduciary responsibility from your employer or plan sponsor. The trustee is in charge of making sure your money gets to the right investment once you have chosen where to invest your account funds.

Plan Administrator

The plan administrator manages the day-to-day operations of your 401(k) account. The plan administrator will also answer your questions.

Record Keeper

The record keeper has information on any withdrawals, contributions, and investments you make with your 401(k) account funds. The record keeper is also in charge of sending your account statements on a quarterly or yearly basis.

Investment Manager

The investment manager is the person in charge of buying and selling the investments you choose.

Keeping Tabs on Your Account

There is no way to stress enough the importance of keeping tabs on your 401(k) account. Even the smallest changes can make a big difference when you retire. The first thing you need to always be aware of is how close you are to the contribution limits so you can make sure not to go over. If you do, you will be penalized. After you make your initial investments (discussed in Chapters 4, 5, and 6) or reallocate your investments (discussed in Chapter 7), make sure your money is properly invested. The account managers who handle your 401(k) dollars make hundreds of investments and are bound to make a mistake at one point or another. Do not accept any mistakes. When you check in on your investments, be sure to also note that you are still receiving employer matching contributions, as long as they are offered and you are eligible to receive them. In addition, while you are looking at your matching funds, be sure to check your vesting status as well to find out whether you are fully vested or nearing that time — see Chapter 2 for more information about vesting and employer matching contributions. If you are not yet fully vested, make a note of when you will be, and ensure that your employer is keeping up with that date.

You should always be keeping track of how your funds are performing so you can determine whether you need to reallocate your account dollars into higher- or lower-risk investments.

Finally, know your fees. You do not want to be overcharged on any account maintenance or other investment fees.

CASE STUDY: HEAD TO HEAD: HOW WORKERS VIEW RETIREMENT

Josh Goodman, 26-year-old journalist
Judy Kleba, 62-year-old financial accountant

Josh: My employer offers a 401(k) retirement savings account, and I participate in it.

Judy: My employer offers a 401(k) retirement account and I participate in it. I also have a pension from a former employer. I used a previous 401(k) to pay for a child's education expenses.

CASE STUDY: HEAD TO HEAD: HOW WORKERS VIEW RETIREMENT

Josh: I decided to participate in the retirement plan when I realized I did not need all of my day-to-day income.

Judy: I figured these retirement accounts would be an easy way of saving since it comes out of my check and it would provide me money in the future.

Josh: My employer offers a matching contribution, but I do not remember what it is.

Judy: My previous employer did not offer matching contributions, but my current one does — they match up to 5 percent of my contributions. Also, if my current company exceeds profits, they divide it out among the employees, but I have not gotten any yet.

Josh: I have not considered how much I will need in retirement.

Judy: I have not considered how much I will need in retirement.

Josh: I consulted with my parents to decide how much to invest, and right now, it is in various asset classes, mostly conservative.

Judy: I have invested in many safe accounts that are recommended for people my age — safe stocks, bonds, and mutual funds. I received a booklet from my employer that helped me reach this decision.

Josh: Once every three months, I check in to see how my investments are doing. I have not felt the need to reallocate yet.

Judy: I get a quarterly statement from my plan. I have not yet reallocated my funds.

Josh: The slow economy has not affected my decisions yet. I still have 40 years until I retire, so short-term economic factors do not seem important to me right now.

Judy: The slow economy has affected me because I cancelled the employer stock I was buying. I increased what I put into the plan, and I am going to increase it again to get closer to the maximum because I only have a few more years to save.

CASE STUDY: HEAD TO HEAD: HOW WORKERS VIEW RETIREMENT

Judy: If I could offer one piece of advice to Josh, it would be to find someone other than your parents to help you with your finances — get a good financial planner or take a seminar about investing and retirement planning. I did not do this over the years, and I regret not doing it or paying more attention to my finances years ago. Because you have 40 years until retirement, you should probably diversify more into riskier investments.

I Need Help

401(k) plans and investments can be overwhelming, but there are places you can go for help. If you are willing to shell out the money, you can get a financial advisor or planner. Otherwise, for free, you can turn to your 401(k) plan holder, your employer (who can offer you investment advice as of 2006), financial Web sites (there are many listed in the Appendix), or even other employees in your office who are also invested in the plan.

The new 2006 pension law provisions allow your employer to give you investment advice through your 401(k) plan provider or a third party without having to worry about being sued after investments do not perform as the employer had thought they would, bringing a substantial change to the retirement market. According to a statement by Tim McCabe, vice president of PMFM Inc., employers will be able to use this advice as an incentive to new employees. "Plans that don't offer investment advice going forward will be the exception rather than the rule." Many employees can stand to benefit from this type of advice because they do not know what they are doing when investing in a retirement plan or whom to go to for help.

The question, then, becomes, whether you should trust your employer to give you good investment advice, especially when you consider the fact that your employer may be linked to certain forms of investments that he or she will want you to put your retirement funds toward. There are some protections built into the new pension law that help stop your employer from taking advantage of you. One stipulation is that any recommendations on where or how you should invest your 401(k) or other retirement account must come from a computer program to ensure that the answer is unbiased. Plus, any fees you are required to pay to receive this advice cannot be put toward any specific investment. Finally, your advisor must tell you, upon request, where he or she gets his or her income from. While these protections should be enough, according to a statement made by PMFM's McCabe, "There will always be a very, very small minority of financial professionals who will break the rules." If you think that you will need advice over an extended time or until you reach retirement, you may want to consider going to a professional investment firm.

If you decide to go to your employer for advice, and you pay half a percent or less of the balance in your 401(k) account, you can consider yourself lucky. Because your employer will be working with an independent subcontractor, he or she may try to recoup his or her fee in whatever you end up paying for the advice. But, whatever your employer charges you through a third party will almost always be less than what you would pay if you went to an independent investment firm.

If you decide that your employee-offered 401(k) plan is not that good, you should almost certainly seek the help of a financial planner. If you like your job, you most likely are not willing to switch jobs just because you do not like the 401(k) or other retirement account offered by your employer. Do not let your employer lure you into a false sense of security by offering numerous bells and whistles that you do not need and that will do nothing more than increase the fees you need to pay on the account. Also, do not just decide to split up all your investments among the different options offered by your employer. You need to make wise decisions, whether you have a subpar account or a wonderful investment plan.

If it does get to a point where you feel you need professional help to manage your 401(k) account, you need to choose your financial advisor wisely. A financial advisor may be known as a wealth-services provider or investment consultant. Anyone you choose to go to for help needs to be a broker, registered investment advisor, or certified financial planner. Look for an advisor who has low commissions and fees. Generally, a fee-only registered investment advisor (RIA) is your best choice.

If you choose to go to a brokerage firm, they have a wealth of information to help you with any planning problem, but that information comes with higher fees. Be sure that you let a broker know your goals and your investment comfort level. Brokerage firms have no fiduciary requirement; they just have to act suitably. With a brokerage firm, you need to prepare yourself to be hands-on with your investments. The broker will ask for the go-ahead at each step, even for a simple investment.

If you are curious about how you can find a good broker, check out Brokercheck, offered by the Financial Industry Regulatory Authority at **www.finra.org**.

Should you decide to go with a registered investment advisor, these people do have fiduciary responsibility to you. They can help you form a comprehensive retirement plan. There are two types of registered investment advisors you can go to — discretionary or nondiscretionary. A discretionary advisor requires a six-figure investment. Someone else will make all the decisions for you, but you will get regular reports on how your investments are performing. Nondiscretionary advisors require approval for each trade but also have lower investment requirements. Both types of advisors will require that you pay a fee based on the assets they manage. Therefore, the better your investments do, the more you will pay.

Pay attention to any potential conflict of interest — some investment companies push their employees to get clients to invest in the company or in stocks beneficial to the company. Do not trust word of mouth when finding your advisor. Also, do not forget to look into each potential advisor and find out whether he or she has been frequently moving from firm to firm. Here are some questions to ask any potential advisor:

- What are your fees?

- Can you show me how you have delivered a high rate of return?

- What kinds of statements or reports will I receive from you? How often will I get them?

- How often will I have contact with you? Do you update me, or do I need to contact you?

- Are you a fiduciary?

- How are you paid? (Make sure your investor is not paid to recommend the company's products.)

- Why have previous clients left your service?

- If I have a problem or complaint, whom do I need to speak with?

- What does your firm offer for dispute resolution?

- Do you have examples of accounts you have previously invested?

- How will we discuss my own level of comfort with investment, and how will that play into the decisions you make for me?

- What resources do you have available to me? What resources do you have available to you that can assist in your decisions about my investments?

Another thing to be mindful of is fixing problems when something seems suspicious to you. If after checking in on your account, you suspect things are not right, and especially if you have noticed multiple problems, stop making contributions immediately. Do not cease contributions if the wrong amount was taken out of your paycheck once; look for bigger problems — incorrect investments, being overcharged on your fees, or unresponsive plan sponsors or investment managers. Talk to your employer and find contact information in your summary plan description to find out who is best to talk to so that the problem can get fixed fast. If the problem is bad enough, look to the federal government and an attorney for help. Check with other employees at your company and see whether they have been recognizing the same problems. If so, consider a class-action suit — you will get attention faster because the federal government likes to see patterns before taking action. When you feel like you need to take drastic steps, contact the IRS, Department of Labor, or Department of Justice.

Department of Labor
Frances Perkins Building
200 Constitution NW Ave.
Washington, DC 20210
Phone: 1-866-4-USA-DOL
www.dol.gov

Internal Revenue Service
Phone: 1-800-829-1040
www.irs.gov

U.S. Department of Justice
950 Pennsylvania NW Ave.
Washington, DC 20530-0001
Phone: 1-202-514-2000
www.usdoj.gov

Warning signs from the Department of Labor that your 401(k) account is being misused:

1. Your 401(k) or individual account statement is consistently late or comes at irregular intervals

2. Your account balance does not appear to be accurate

3. Your employer failed to transmit your contribution to the plan on a timely basis

4. A significant drop in account balance that cannot be explained by normal market ups and downs

5. 401(k) or individual account statement shows your contribution from your paycheck was not made

6. Investments listed on your statement are not what you authorized

7. Former employees are having trouble getting their benefits paid on time or in the correct amounts

8. Unusual transactions, such as a loan to the employer, a corporate officer, or one of the plan trustees

9. Frequent and unexplained changes in investment managers or consultants

10. Your employer has recently experienced severe financial difficulty

Tips from the Department of Labor, Employee Benefits Security Administration

www.dol.gov/ebsa/publications/10warningsigns.html

Action Item

Be sure that your financial advisor is a fiduciary:

1. Attorneys, certified public accountants, and registered investment advisors are fiduciaries

2. Certified financial planners and financial planners might be fiduciaries

3. Insurance agents, registered representatives, and stock brokers are not fiduciaries

---

Action Item

What do you need to ask to figure out whether a possible financial planner is a fiduciary?

1. Are you legally bound to act in my best interest and willing to put that in writing?

2. Are there any conflicts of interest I should be aware of? Will you let me know if any arise?

3. How will I pay you?

If the financial advisor you are considering is legitimate, they have to have filed Form ADV with the Securities and Exchange Commission. You can find these on the SEC's Web site. Unfortunately, conflict-of-interest information contained in the ADV must be obtained from the adviser you are considering.

What Should You Do If Something Is Not Offered?

Different employers at different companies offer different 401(k) investment options and features. There are many benefits your employer could add to the 401(k) plan he or she offers, but often, they will not until someone steps up and asks for it. If you are with a company that has major direct competition, you have obvious leverage in asking your employer for another benefit. Call up similar companies and find out what their 401(k) plans offer. If they have a benefit you would like to see added to the plan, tell your boss that you are considering changing jobs because of better 401(k) options at another company. Better yet, form a group in your office of concerned individuals and lobby your boss all at once.

There are some up-and-coming benefits in 401(k) plans that are important for you to know about. One is the Roth 401(k). According to *Money* magazine, only about one-quarter of employers offer this type of plan, but it can be beneficial for people in a higher tax bracket (for more information on tax brackets, see Chapter 1). The Roth 401(k) only allows after-tax contributions, but this means you will not be taxed when you end up making withdrawals after retirement. Another benefit is the addition of a service that can automatically reallocate your investment funds for you. If your plan offers this, rebalancing of your account to improve performance happens about four times per year and tends to be free. Target-date funds can also be a good investment. We will talk more about this type of fund in Chapter 5, but for now, all you need to know is that this fund invests your money and rebalances until you retire, gradually moving you from high-risk investments to more conservative options. Finally, ask your employer whether your 401(k) plan offers any professional investment advice. Many companies have begun offering this service for free to interested employees.

Chapter 3 Summary

- Before you sign up for your 401(k) account, and while you have the account open, you will receive multiple documents from your employer, 401(k) plan administrator, and any investment company you are working with. Be sure to keep, read, and understand all documents given to you.

- If you do not understand something, there are many places you can find help — your employer can offer assistance, other employees in your office may be able to answer some simple questions, and many investment brokers offer free, wide-ranging education help to anyone, even if you do not have an investment account with them.

- There are multiple people that help to administer your 401(k) plan. Be sure to know who each person is, what they do, and how you can get in contact with them in the event that something goes wrong or if you just want to check in to see how your account is doing.

- There are many beneficial offerings your employer can put into the 401(k) plan. If he or she does not offer something you feel like you would like to see in your plan, just ask for it. Better yet, get a bunch of the employees together and ask your employer what he or she can offer you. Understand and hold on to the summary plan description, plan prospectus (for mutual fund holders), and plan statement.

- Keep records on your 401(k) account and check in periodically. Because this is a long-term investment strategy, you should not plan to check in too often because you will scare yourself away from investing and will want to constantly change your investment strategy with every little dip in the market, but look in periodically to change your investment strategy, if necessary, and make sure your money is invested the way you want it to be.

- If you decide to get help, look to people in your office, your investment holders, and others for advice. If you choose to seek professional help, choose wisely, and be sure you are aware of the fees you will need to pay and how they will be charged, and be sure whomever you hire is credible and can provide examples of previous service.

4 *Investing Basics and Stocks*

In this chapter, you will learn:

- What different investment options are available

- All about investing in and choosing stocks

Now that you have everything set up, it is time to start building your nest egg and making some serious money for retirement. There are many investment options you need to consider, including mutual funds, money market funds, guaranteed investment contracts, bond funds, balanced funds, company stock, international funds, and stocks; your employer may limit the type of funds you are able to invest in. Any investments you make are dependent on how much risk you can handle. If you are just joining the workforce at a young age, you can handle more risk and the ups and downs of the economy. If you are nearing retirement, you cannot handle much risk because you will be withdrawing your money in the near future and will not be able to ride out a financial downturn.

When you are considering your investments, you must look at the expected rate of return. This means looking at how the investment has performed in the past and then making an educated guess about how it will perform in the future. One warning from financial advisors, though, is that past performance does not always indicate future performance. You must take into account the current market situation and how a certain industry might perform in the future.

The estimated return on your investment is important for your retirement planning. When you sit down to figure out how much you will need in retirement, this number will help guide you in choosing investments based on their potential rate of return. If you consider the amount that you will contribute to your account annually, how many years you will spend in retirement, and how much you will receive from your investments, you will get a good picture of exactly how much you will make before retirement — and if you stick with this formula, you will have this amount to live off of in retirement. If you decide that you cannot contribute enough to earn what you need in retirement, you will have to put your money in well-diversified, higher-risk investments to receive a higher return.

There are many different investments you can consider; one genre is known as cash or cash equivalents. These types of investments include bank savings accounts and certificates of deposit (CDs), which require that any money you deposit into them remain there for a stated period; when you are able to withdraw your money, you will get a specified interest rate. The longer your money is in a CD, and the more money you have invested in it, the more you stand to make when you pull the money out of it. A money market deposit account is another type of cash equivalent investment that is essentially a bank account that requires a minimum deposit and balance; otherwise, you will be penalized. This type of account commonly does better than a savings account but worse than a CD. The money market deposit account can be purchased from a bank and is insured by the FDIC. U.S. Treasury Bills (T-bills) are for short-term cash investments that come in lengths of three months, six months, or one year; you can buy them in increments of $10,000. Series EE bonds (or savings bonds) offer tax-free earnings and have come and gone in popularity. The Guaranteed Investment Contract (or GIC) is like a CD but is purchased from an insurance company through your 401(k) plan. You will be guaranteed an interest rate, and it is not insured through the federal government. With a GIC, you will not earn enough over time to outpace inflation.

There are some good terms to be aware of when it comes to stocks. The price-earnings ratio (P/E ratio) will let you know if a stock is overpriced. The P/E ratio is calculated by dividing the stock's current price by its earnings. If the ratio is high, the stock is most likely overvalued. Market capitalization (cap) is based on how large a company's stock price is. If you multiply the market price of the stock and the total number of outstanding shares, you will arrive at the market cap. This number is used to identify small-, mid-, and large-cap stocks, but there is no clear definition; the distinction will vary from company to company.

Another investment choice is bonds. Bonds are essentially loans. You are lending money to the issuer

— be it a company or a government entity — with the promise of getting a fixed interest rate along with your initial investment back when your bond reaches its maturity date.

Bond Term
Face value (otherwise known as par value) is the original amount you invest in the bond. You will receive all of this back when your bond reaches maturity. Some bonds have a stipulation that the company does not need to wait until the maturity date to give you your money and can pay off what they owe you before full maturity is reached. The maturity date is the day the issuer of your bond promises to repay your principal and any interest you have earned. Coupon is the interest paid until your bond reaches maturity.

Bonds can come in many forms — U.S. government securities, Treasury bonds, corporate bonds, municipal bonds, or zero-coupon bonds.

When investing your 401(k) retirement account funds, you can choose a mutual fund, which is a combination of different stocks and bonds. Your money is pooled and invested by professionals. You do not have to invest too much into a mutual fund. There are a few different types of mutual funds you can choose to invest in: stock mutual funds, bond mutual funds, and money market mutual funds, which should not be confused with money market deposit accounts.

Another investment option is stocks, otherwise known as equities. With a stock, you purchase a piece of a company. This chapter will discuss stocks in more detail.

The first thing you should do is figure out how to allocate your funds among asset classes. A pie chart is a good way to figure out the different percentages you will put toward each asset class.

Action Item
Do not compare the performance of different types of asset classes — you cannot compare stocks with bonds and vice versa. Stocks can only be compared to other stocks.

When thinking about how to allocate your funds among asset classes, also consider the risk involved in the other savings you will have in retirement — for example, a guaranteed pension is a safer plan, which would allow you to invest your 401(k) money more aggressively than you might have if you did not have a pension. The same principle goes for company stock — if you get it for free, it is a high-risk investment, so spend your money on lower-risk investments.

The Department of Labor indicates to your employer the type of information that you must receive about your investment options in order to allow you to make educated decisions about your investments. This includes a description of each option, including the risk and return on each, who the investment managers are in case you have questions or concerns, how you can change your investment choices and when you can do that, what fees you will be charged for various reasons, and the fiduciary's contact information.

Fast Fact

If a stock or other investment looks like it has abnormally high returns, it is probably too good to be true. It might continue strong, but it will most likely drop significantly in the near future.

Action Item

When trying to figure out what your return should be, think about how much you could lose in a quarter (your risk tolerance) and divide that by two. Add a money market rate to this, and the number you come out with should be your rate of growth over a decade.

Fast Fact

Even some of the brightest people make common mistakes with their retirement plan — do not worry if you are not a financial scholar.

Fast Fact

Do not fear being wrong in the decisions you make about your retirement or retirement investments; there is no way you can know absolutely what is going to happen. The best you can do is make educated guesses; it is important to learn something about what you are about to embark on.

Investments for Everyone

Investing your 401(k) account dollars is important because you need to beat inflation. Each year, as inflation rises and the value of the dollar changes, the money you have in a bank account will be worth less when you retire than it is now. To beat the rising inflation, you need to choose wise investments.

Different investors will recommend multiple types of 401(k) account fund allocation. Some may suggest that you invest more in bonds, while others prefer stocks. The key is to consider what you are most comfortable with, how long you have until retirement, and what your goals are in retirement, all while you continue in the job force. While investing your 401(k) plan is certainly not one-size-fits-all, there are some common guidelines that the average investor can follow. These guidelines will not apply to everyone but can be used as stepping stones on which to build your knowledge of investing.

When you are just getting started at work and in investing, mainly those between the ages of 25 and 40, you will want to think about whether you need to be conservative (if you cannot tolerate too much risk based on personal preference), moderate (if you just want to try and get your feet wet and feel your way through investing), or aggressive (if you can stomach the changes in the market). If you choose to invest in a more conservative manner, about 75 percent of what you invest should be in some type of growth or income fund — there will be less risk and, therefore, less return, but you will have a more stable account. The other 25 percent can be divided between bond funds. Bond funds not only add diversification to your account, but they also create stability. Should you choose to go with a moderate investment plan when you start out, 80 percent of your funds should go to stock funds that are growth-oriented, while the other 20 percent should go into some form of bond fund. Finally, if you want to be aggressive, put 15 or so percent into bond funds; 25 percent into stock funds held by smaller companies, which have more potential for growth; 30 percent into the stock funds of large companies, which tend to be far more stable; and 30 percent into international funds, which will significantly diversify your account because you will be invested in a market that does not necessarily track with the domestic market.

If you are drawing closer to retirement, between the ages of 40 and 55, this is the time when you want to sit down and carefully consider what you will need once you retire and whether you are on track to get there. Again, you can choose to be a conservative, moderate, or aggressive investor, but the difference here is that you will not have the luxury to be as aggressive as you were when you were younger, which may mean smaller returns. If you choose to go with a more conservative investment, you will want to keep about 10 percent of your account funds in a government-backed investment — these are the most stable investments because no matter what you think of the government, they are required to come through on the money they owe to the public. Another 30 percent can be allocated to bond funds — both short and intermediate — with more money going toward intermediate funds.

Finally, the remaining 60 percent of your 401(k) account funds should be invested in small-company funds, international growth funds, or growth and income funds. Should you decide that you want to be a moderate saver, you want to put about one-third of your 401(k) account funds toward bond funds, be they from companies or the federal government (depending on what level of stability you want for that), and the remaining two-thirds should go toward growth funds — either international or domestic — or income stocks and bonds. Should you choose to go with an aggressive investment stance, you will want to have a stable 10 percent spread out between corporate and government bonds, 10 percent in international bonds, 25 percent in small-company stock funds for added growth, another 25 percent in international stock funds for good diversification, and 30 percent in quality growth funds.

A Tip from Vanguard

An investment strategy can serve as your emotional anchor and help you feel more confident about your choices because you know you have a well-balanced, well-thought-out plan. You do not need many different investments to achieve excellent diversification. A few broadly based index funds, or life cycle and balanced funds (which invest in both stocks and bonds in one fund), can provide the appropriate level. Sometimes, the best solutions are the simplest.

Once you reach that threshold when you are on the verge of retirement, between the ages of 55 and 65 (or even older if you have decided to work longer), you will unquestionably be shifting to more conservative investments on the whole, whether you choose to go with the conservative, moderate, or aggressive investment pattern. Conservative investors will put 15 percent of their 401(k) account funds into international funds, 15 percent into short-term corporate bonds, 15 percent into an intermediate-term bond, 20 percent into bonds backed by the U.S. government, and 35 percent into growth funds. If you choose to stick with a more moderate investment strategy, 15 percent should go into funds backed by the U.S. government, 30 percent mixed between short and intermediate bond funds, 15 percent in international funds, and the final 40 percent should go into some form of growth or income fund. Finally, when you invest aggressively, you will want to keep about 30 percent in bonds and spread it out between intermediate-term, international, and short-term bonds. Another 10 percent of your 401(k) account funds can go into a government-backed investment, 15 percent can go into riskier international stocks, and the final 45 percent can go into domestic funds.

Even if there are currently high returns, you should never take these into account when planning your retirement or expect that the high returns will continue until your retirement — abnormally high returns come around occasionally but not often enough that you will be able to plan for them.

All investments carry some form of risk, and if you do not properly diversify your 401(k) investments, you are at risk of losing more than you would like to, or more than you can afford. This is rare, however, as long as you take the time and care to wisely choose investments and diversify to protect yourself from unnecessary loss.

A Tip from Vanguard

Keep it simple, maximize diversification, minimize costs, and start with a plan. With the media full of ads touting recent performance, investors can be tempted to drift from one fund to the next. When temptation wins, the culprit is typically the lack of a comprehensive investment strategy. Investors without a well-thought-out strategy to guide their choices tend to collect funds based solely on the latest performance figures. Taking this fragmented approach may lead you to invest excessively in parts of the market that have outperformed recently at the expense of the underperforming areas. In doing so, you might accumulate many funds, but you could still lack adequate diversification, as those funds are likely to have overlapping holdings.

A Tip from ShareBuilder

Keep it simple; complexity is not your friend. Start with a few broad-based index funds — for example, one that tracks the S&P 500 — or a model portfolio that fits your investment style (i.e., conservative, moderate, or aggressive). Do not get overwhelmed by all the investment choices and hot stocks of the moment. There is a reason that Warren Buffet promotes indexing approach for most investors — the market is hard to beat. Keep it simple, and you will be much more confident in how you do over time. Also, take advantage of the match in your 401(k) plan, if you have access to one. It is like a bonus that can significantly add up over time.

Stocks

When you purchase a stock, you are purchasing ownership in a company. How much you make off your investment is dependent on how well the company does. Stocks have the highest potential for return, but there is also high risk involved because of the volatility of the stock market, which serves as a validation to an earlier point: 401(k)s are not quick fixes. You have to be in it for a long time, or you stand to lose a good amount of money — especially in stocks — because prices rise and fall every day, depending on each specific company and on the overall state of the economy. One thing to bear in mind, though, is that market cycles are normal — there will be good times and bad.

A good strategy to take part in when it comes to stocks is dollar-cost averaging. Dollar-cost averaging is essentially investing money in your 401(k) account on a set schedule so that you will sometimes buy stocks low and sometimes buy stocks high, but eventually, this will balance itself out. Industry analysts commonly say that with dollar-cost averaging, investors buy more shares when they are low for a better return on investment. For the most part, you do not need to do anything special to take advantage of dollar-cost averaging — if you are contributing to your 401(k) account, you are already participating in this benefit.

Some financial advisors will tell you to invest all your money in stocks, and if you can stand the risk, and do not need your 401(k) to get by in retirement, an argument could be made for this scenario. Yet, 60 percent in stocks and 40 percent in bonds is normally the safest. If you are young, or even in your 40s or 50s, you can stand to have most of your money in stocks, especially if you do not plan to withdraw the money from your 401(k) account right away when you retire.

When choosing between stocks and bonds, take note that since 1962, stocks have returned an annual 10 percent, bonds returned 5 percent, and cash investments returned just 4 percent, according to the research-investment firm, Ibbotson Associates. If you take inflation into consideration, stocks returned 7 percent annually, bonds returned 2 percent, and cash returned 1 percent. Each decade — even including the years during the Great Depression — stocks have never lost more than 1 percent annually. Plus, when any two decades are taken together, stocks have not lost at all. While the stock market seems like a risky place to invest for your future, the key is longevity. If you plan to have long-term investments, stocks are actually a safe, high-returning investment. Bonds, on the other hand, tend to have a lower, more even rate of return and, therefore, have less risk.

Over time, each of the different types of stock take a turn being the best in the market — some boom for years and quickly drop off, while others start slowly and boom suddenly. During the past five years, according to Kiplinger's, funds that invest in some of the largest-growing companies have not been doing well, while the funds that deal with small- and medium-sized companies have been experiencing significant growth, which translates into a good return for investors. Now, however, the market seems to be taking a turn back to favoring those larger companies.

To best diversify your stock holdings, you will want to have at least one fund that invests in smaller companies because those have historically provided the best returns — of course, these funds also have some of the most risk because of the volatility of small companies. So, you will also need to have some room in your portfolio for stock in larger companies, which provide a more stable but lower rate of return over the years. Another good balance is to look for growth and value stocks — growth stocks are in a period of quick growth and large profits, while value stocks are often cheaper and are not growing as fast. Kiplinger's suggests that the money you invest in stocks should be split as follows — 50 percent in large companies, with some money toward growth stocks and some toward value stocks; 25 percent of your stock investments in foreign funds; and another 25 percent split between small companies that are considered either growth or value stocks.

One of the best ways to invest in the stock market is to purchase a total stock market index fund. But another option is to go with a sector-specific fund, which will invest your money only in technologies, for example. While this will help to diversify your portfolio, you need to be prepared for some excellent — and awful — years. Sector funds tend to swing from good to bad rapidly.

A Tip from ShareBuilder

Stocks are an important part of anybody's portfolio. Stocks, as an asset class, are the most volatile, but they have had the greatest returns over time, and the return advantage over bonds and cash has historically been more than just a little. There are no guarantees, but to meet your goals and overcome that tyrant known as inflation, stocks make sense for almost everyone. How close you are to retirement and your personal comfort with the market swings are the key considerations. If you cannot sleep at night when the market goes down, and you are close to retirement, you may only want 10 to 20 percent in stocks. If you are young, and severe market swings are something you take in stride, 80 to 90 percent in stocks may be right for you.

Types of Stocks

There are various types of stocks you can purchase and much terminology that surrounds them. The following are some basic ideas you should familiarize yourself with if you decide to invest in stocks yourself. "Cap" is short for market capitalization, which is calculated by multiplying the number of shares outstanding at a company by the price per share. The cap size is not a strict rule — for one reason or another, some companies may be classified outside of the category they appear to fit in.

- **Mega-cap stocks:** The stock of a company with a market capitalization greater than $200 billion.

- **Large-cap (big-cap) stocks:** The stock of a company with a market capitalization greater than $10 billion.

- **Mid-cap stocks:** The sock of a company with a market capitalization between $2 billion and $10 billion.

- **Small-cap stocks:** The stock of a company with a market capitalization between $300 million and $2 billion.

- **Micro-cap stocks:** The stock of a company with a market capitalization between $50 million and $300 million.

- **Nano-cap stocks:** the stock of a company with a market capitalization less than $50 million.

- **Growth stocks:** Company stock with a value that is expected to grow at an above-average rate over time. This term generally applies to stock held in technology companies.

- **Value stocks:** A company's stock being sold for less than it is worth.

- **Blue-chip stocks:** Stocks held in the largest, most established companies. They are considered more stable than other stocks. The companies listed in the Dow Jones Industrial Average are blue-chip stocks.

- **Income stocks:** A stock that has paid high dividends over time.

- **Employer stocks:** Stocks you may be able to purchase or receive from your employer, which allow you to own a portion of the company you work for.

Employer Stocks

The larger your company, the more likely it is to offer some form of company stock for you to purchase or invest your 401(k) retirement plan in. This is considered one of the most risky choices of all stock investments, especially if you have too much company stock in your portfolio, because how much your investment will return is dependent on the performance of your company, and you do not want to be double invested in a company — you do not want a situation where they control your salary and a majority of your 401(k) fund. Employer stocks are also bad news for the simple reason that all single stocks are not a good investment idea — when the performance of that one company is bad, all your earnings will be bad because you have too much invested in one place. With diversification of many stocks, in the event that one company performs poorly, you will have the other companies, which may be having a better year, to help even out your earnings. Of course, you could say that you work for a large, strong company and should not have to worry about them going under. But these days, even the big companies can suffer downsizing, mergers, or other financial troubles. Take, for example, the problem with Enron in 2000, where employees lost significant portions of their retirement accounts because so much of the fund was invested in employer stocks. When you are a stockholder, you are vulnerable to the actions of the company and the company's managers. Of course, company stock can offer diversification if used wisely and purchased in small increments.

Some companies force their employees to purchase company stock or only make matching contributions in the form of company stock. You would be better off to avoid a company like this — it will give you no control over how your retirement funds are invested. If you find yourself unable to avoid this position, make an effort to diversify your portfolio, especially with investments in lower-risk stocks and bonds. Sometimes, especially large companies will give you your matching funds in the form of company stock because they believe you will take pride in your job and company and work harder. Some employers also believe that giving an employee company stock is a gesture of good faith, indicating that the company will continue to perform well.

The Pension Protection Act of 2006 now requires employers to let their employees cash out company stock within three years of receiving it for diversification purposes. Many employers have gone above and beyond the act's requirements and allowed employees to transfer out of the company stock plan at any time.

There is a possibility that you can lose quite a bit of your retirement money if you have too much invested in company stock — if your company goes bankrupt, you will probably lose the money invested there. If your employer offers you company stock, you should take it and use it as a means of diversification, but try not to invest too much of your own money into the company.

International Stocks

International stock funds invest in companies outside of the United States. According to Investopedia, a Forbes Media Company, U.S. stocks make up only half of the value of all global markets, and there are more than 20 major markets outside of the United States. Commonly, this is seen as one of the higher-risk investments and is best for young investors. Because of its high risk, it also has the potential for a high rate of return and can be used to properly balance a portfolio that also includes domestic stocks. Foreign markets run in cycles just like our domestic market, but they run opposite each other. When domestic markets are in a downturn, foreign markets tend to be performing well and vice versa. This is not always true, because there are countries that depend on the goods and services made in the United States; any country faced with this situation will have an economy that mirrors that of the United States.

There are multiple types of international funds, and you choose them based on their risk and the amount of risk you can handle. One of the riskiest investments is buying stock in companies located in Third World or developing nations.

Before making the decision to invest in international stocks, do your research. It is important to recognize the risk involved in any specific country or region you plan to invest in. The U.S. dollar fluctuates in value all around the world, and it is imperative that whatever stock you choose to invest in has a currency that is strong against the dollar. Any weakening value of the local currency will cause your return to drop. You also want to be mindful of any social, political, or economic turmoil going on in any country you plan to invest in. Given these tips on risk, it is safest to invest in stocks in European nations.

There are steps you can take that will allow you to invest in foreign markets but still have some of the safety and security of the U.S. economy. You have three choices in this realm: American Depositary Receipts, U.S. Traded International Stocks, and U.S. Multinationals (such as McDonald's).

Fast Fact

Why invest internationally? There are generally higher returns, and it helps you diversify your currency holdings (in case the dollar is weak).

How Is My Stock Performing?

If you are curious about how your stocks are performing, you need to look at an index. An index is an indication of how the market as a whole is doing. It is an average that tracks how securities are performing. One of the most popular indexes is the Dow Jones Industrial Average, which tracks only 30 stocks, but they are some of the largest, blue-chip stocks on the market. What you need to find is an index that fits your needs and reflects the stocks you hold. Dow Jones is good for people who hold stocks in many large companies. Another popular index, the S&P 500, does not include small-cap stocks. Smaller stocks can be found on the Wilshire Small-Cap Index or the Russell 2000 Index. NASDAQ is also a good place to look for small-cap stocks because it follows thousands of stocks of varying sizes, which will show more volatility than the 30 Dow stocks, meaning you will get a better overview of the market as a whole. The S&P 400 Mid-Cap Index looks at mid-cap stocks. Foreign stocks can be tracked on the index known as the Morgan Stanley Capital International Europe, Australia, Far East Index. The downside to this index is that it does not include any Latin American stocks and is heavily weighted toward Japan. If you need to check in on a balanced fund or asset allocation fund that invests in both small and large stocks, you should look to the Wilshire 5000 Index, which tracks 5,000 stocks — all the major ones of all sizes. A good place to look for a listing of the indexes each day is *The Wall Street Journal*.

Fast Fact

A common rule when investing is that if you do not fully understand an investment, do not make it. There are too many variables involved that you will not understand or be able to make wise decisions about.

Chapter 4 Summary

- Look closely at the estimated rate of return on the investments you are considering, but remember that past performance does not guarantee future performance.

- There are multiple investment options, each with its own risk factors, but the more risk you take on, the more you have the potential to earn.

- Some options for investing your 401(k) account are mutual funds, CDs, bonds, and stocks.

- Some investments are better for people at certain ages, and sometimes you are better off having more money in these specific investments at a certain age. Younger people want more money in stocks because they will gain the most, but young people also have the longest time available to bounce back from any market losses.

- There are many different types of stocks—including individual companies and your own employer.

- Choose stocks wisely — do not just follow the herd or immediately invest in whichever company is currently doing the best. Try to invest in many different types of companies and sectors to add stability to your portfolio.

- Be wary of holding too much company stock — you do not want to place your current earnings and your future lifestyle in the hands of a single company.

5 Investing in Mutual Funds and Bonds

In this chapter, you will learn:

- About investing in mutual funds
- The various forms of bonds and which type is best for you

Mutual Funds

Mutual funds are a beneficial addition to any 401(k) investment portfolio. They offer diversification and can add risk or stability, depending on what type you choose. The mutual funds that perform best over time often charge lower fees and will have some of the most experienced fund managers, according to Standard & Poor's Mutual Fund Performance Persistence Scorecard. Like any investment, you can lose money in a mutual fund, but how much is dependent on what type you choose. Plus, as with most other investments, the federal government does not protect or insure the plan, so choose wisely — your investments are only as good as the company that holds them.

A mutual fund is a company investment program where you invest your 401(k) account funds in, which will combine your money with money from other investors and use it to purchase stocks, bonds, money market funds, and others. You benefit because you do not need to choose stocks and bonds on your own — the company, as long as it is reputable, will make wise investment decisions for you.

When you invest in a mutual fund, you will receive a prospectus that outlines everything you need to know about your mutual fund. Be sure to read and understand it. Your mutual fund investment manager is required by law to give you the prospectus before you choose to invest in the fund. Normally, the prospectus will be easy to understand, but if there are any investment terms you are unsure of, be sure to call your mutual fund manager before you sign the paperwork. Some of the information included in the prospectus includes what the fund seeks to do, including: its goal; long-term investment strategy; what types of people should invest in the particular mutual fund you are looking into; any fees you will be charged when you invest in the mutual fund; the value of your shares at the end of each year; how the fund has performed over time; and the basics on setting up your mutual fund account.

Like any other investment, there are advantages and disadvantages to any investment. Mutual funds offer the benefit of professional investors (as long as you choose a mutual fund wisely) and added diversification without having to make many bond or stock picks yourself. Some mutual funds are cheap to buy into, and, by and large, you can decide to pull your money out of a mutual fund at any time, but you should focus on long-term results as much as possible. Disadvantages include a lack of control in choosing what the mutual fund invests in — if you are new to investing or do not want to take the time to figure out individual investments, then this disadvantage does not apply to you; fees need to be paid whether you make or lose money in the mutual fund; and while you can get a broad idea of performance, you will not necessarily know how much it will cost to buy or sell shares of your mutual fund over time because they have invested in so many different types of funds.

You should know from the outset that, as with stocks, the way a mutual fund has performed in the past does not necessarily dictate how it will perform in the future. Companies and the economy change. There will be fees when you invest in a mutual fund — much like any other investment — so just be aware of them, and know how they will affect the return on your investment. Before investing in any mutual fund, think about where you are in life and what you need out of your retirement investments. Do you need to be conservative, or can you tolerate more risk? There is risk with any mutual fund because as interest rates increase, bond values fall.

For those getting closer to retirement, money market funds are your best choice of mutual funds because they have relatively low risk as required by law. Money markets are quality investments issued by federal or local governments and U.S. companies. These funds try to keep the share purchase price to $1. Money market funds are for people looking for shorter-term investments. Because of the low risk, return is not high, and in a wildly fluctuating market, if inflation outpaces your return, you could be hurt in the end. This scenario, though, is rare.

A second mutual fund investment option is the bond fund. Bond funds have a higher risk, mainly because there is no Securities and Exchange Commission (SEC) restriction on what the bond fund is able to invest in. The added risk is because some bond funds invest in U.S. government or Treasury funds, which have little risk, but other bond funds invest in individual companies that may go under for a number of reasons. The longer your mutual fund holds a company bond, the higher the risk because there is more chance of the company failing. Bonds may also be paid off early, reducing your final return.

You can consider investing in money market mutual funds. This type of investment has a higher rate of return than a simple bank account with low risk but a lower rate of return than many stock funds or bond funds, and you are able to write checks from your investments. Money market funds can come in the form of government or tax-exempt funds. Government funds hold Treasury bills, while tax-exempt money market funds invest in municipal bonds issued by state and local government entities.

The highest-risk mutual fund investments are stock funds, otherwise known as equity funds. Stock funds, as their name implies, invest in stocks. The prices of stocks fluctuate wildly over time, though if you invest for the long-term, any dips will normally even themselves out. There are multiple forms of stock funds, including aggressive growth, income, index, and sector funds. Aggressive growth funds are high-risk but have the potential for a high rate of return on your investment. Aggressive growth funds are invested in companies that look like they have the potential to grow quickly and exponentially — like technology companies during the tech boom. Growth funds have the potential to grow tremendously, though not as quickly as aggressive growth funds. Income funds hold stocks that pay regular dividends — payments to shareholders — and are, therefore, considered more stable because of their ability to pay. Index funds invest in a specific sampling of the market, such as the S&P 500 — which contains only the stocks of 500 large-cap corporations — or a sampling of an entire market to offer more diversification and stability. Finally, sector funds invest in a specific area of the market, such as technology stocks.

A mutual fund is much like having a professional retirement planner working for you — the company makes the best decisions possible about what to invest in based on their goals laid out in the prospectus you will receive. Major mutual fund companies will offer various index funds for you to purchase, or you can choose exchange traded funds from brokers or mutual fund companies. The most common types of index funds are Diamonds, representing companies on the Dow Jones; SPDRs, representing the S&P 500; and QQQs, representing many different segments of the economy.

Fast Fact

ETFs can be sold at any time during the day — there will be extra fees involved because you have to go through a broker, who will charge you for buying and selling shares, but administrative costs may be lower.

A Tip from ShareBuilder

Often, people want to be diversified and choose mutual funds or exchange-traded funds (ETFs) in their retirement plans — we think that is a good choice versus just a single stock or two. We think the smart choice for most investors is to select index-based funds, like ETFs, as the core of the retirement holdings. While there is no guarantee of any investment's future performance, index funds tend to have lower costs and have outperformed the majority of actively managed mutual funds. While you cannot control fund performance, you can help control costs by looking for low-expense ratio funds that align with your objectives.

Balanced Funds

A balanced fund is a form of mutual fund that invests in stocks, bonds, and cash. This has low risk and, therefore, has low yield to invest your retirement account money, but it can be good for new investors, people seeking more stability in their diversified portfolio, and those who do not want to take the time to research other, more specific investment options. The target-date fund is a form of balanced funds.

Target-date Funds

One of the newest types of investments being offered to many 401(k) account holders is the target-date retirement fund or life cycle fund. The idea behind this type of investment is simple: You look at a calendar and pick a realistic date that you want to retire on. Figure out how many years away from this date you are at the time of your investment, and look through the investment options offered by your employer to find the mutual fund that matches this year — these funds normally come in five-year increments. For example, choose a 15-year target date retirement fund if you invest in 2015 and plan to retire in 2030. Instead of having to constantly check on your investments and rebalance as necessary, the fund automatically adjusts your risk based on your age and makes adjustments based on the performance of the investment. If you hold a target-date fund, you are automatically invested into a mix of high- and low-risk investments, including cash, bonds, stocks, and even foreign stocks (for the highest risk).

A Tip from Principal Financial Group

When choosing a target-date fund, pick the option that is closest to your expected retirement date. Do not try to mix and match two or more of the target-dated funds together to make up a different allocation. Once an investor knows which fund to invest in, there is no upkeep. The portfolio managers of the Principal LifeTime portfolios run a well-diversified, institutional-quality, target-date portfolio designed to help investors over their entire lifetime.

One necessary thing to remember is that these are not one-size-fits-all plans. They are set to the "average" person. Therefore, if you have multiple retirement accounts, a large pension plan, or want to work during retirement, it is necessary to take these things into account and decide whether the target-date fund is for you.

A Tip from Vanguard

Vanguard recommends target-date funds; in fact, Vanguard's Target Retirement Funds have been popular with investors. These funds may be most useful for investors who are looking for a straightforward investment vehicle to help them save for retirement, as an alternative to building a portfolio on their own. These funds start with a high-equity allocation for younger investors when their tolerance for risk may be high, and their investment portfolio balances may be smaller than later in life. Then, in a predictable fashion, the equity allocation will moderate over time. This feature, called "automatic allocation adjustment," is consistently noted by investors as a favorite feature. There is nothing about these products that could be construed as "harmful" for any investor, but these products are not intended for investors seeking an asset allocation that will not change (often called target-risk funds) or for investors looking to tailor their portfolio to meet specific objectives or strategies. Target-date funds serve as an important investment option for a large segment of the investor universe.

CASE STUDY: MICHAEL FINNEGAN, CHIEF INVESTMENT OFFICER AND LIFETIME PORTFOLIO MANAGER

Principal Financial Group
711 High Street, Des Moines, IA 50392
www.principal.com
1-800-986-3343 – Voice
Michael Finnegan, Chief Investment
Officer and LifeTime Portfolio Manager

In a target date fund, the strategies were designed to capitalize on the growing popularity of the "do-it-for-me" concept in the defined contribution marketplace. The Principal LifeTime portfolios provide investors access to well-diversified portfolios that automatically reduce key financial risks as the investor's time horizon decreases. The investment options are usually managed over time toward a particular target horizon: usually the investor's estimated retirement date. The options usually invest in various funds, but some options invest directly in stocks and bonds to set the allocation.

CASE STUDY: MICHAEL FINNEGAN, CHIEF INVESTMENT OFFICER AND LIFETIME PORTFOLIO MANAGER

The Principal LifeTime portfolios offer a "fund-of-fund" solution. Each portfolio reflects what the managers believe to be an optimal asset class mix — a combination of equity, fixed income, and real estate — for the respective target date.

Principal LifeTime portfolios series consists of distinct options staged in five-year increments. Like other target-date life cycle offerings, each Principal LifeTime portfolio gradually becomes more conservative as the investor ages. Principal has a set path that is intended to cover the entire expected life of the investor.

We believe that the average investor does not have the time, knowledge, or research capabilities to choose among all the investment options made available to them. Target-date funds are managed by investment professionals that have the knowledge to set an asset allocation based on the investor's expected retirement date. The use of target-date funds has been increasing rapidly, and we view this as a positive development. We feel that more investors could benefit from these strategies.

When investing in a target-date fund, an investor is generally diversified across multiple asset classes, investment styles, and, in the case of Principal LifeTime portfolios, multiple managers. This helps mitigate much of the individual security risk that is embedded in investing in an individual stock or bond.

Principal LifeTime funds leverage our expertise in asset allocation, manager selection, and oversight to offer a comprehensive approach to investing. Our strategies incorporate a wide range of asset classes and investment styles in a "fund-of-funds" structure. We advocate broad diversification, including exposure to traditional asset classes: domestic, international, and broad fixed-income, as well as non-traditional asset classes, income-oriented real estate investments, high-yield, preferred securities, and inflation protection.

Principal LifeTime portfolios embody the following key attributes:

- Broad diversification across multiple traditional and specialty asset classes

CASE STUDY: MICHAEL FINNEGAN, CHIEF INVESTMENT OFFICER AND LIFETIME PORTFOLIO MANAGER

- Professional investment advisors representing a wide range of asset classes, investment styles, and money management firms
- A structured investment process with disciplined risk management at each stage of the investment process

The average investor will benefit the most from a target-date fund. The Principal LifeTime portfolios embrace a multi-asset class, multi-style, and multi-manager approach similar to institutional investment programs, such as corporate- and public-defined benefit plans and large endowments and foundations. Investors with special needs or atypical risk profiles benefit the least from target-date funds.

Tips from Principal Financial Group

- Time and expertise in the financial market is something that most investors do not have. If individuals are going to try and put together their own asset allocation, whether it is individual stocks and bonds or funds, they need to monitor the portfolio and make necessary changes. Target-date funds take care of the allocation and rebalancing for the investor. As always, Principal recommends that an investor start contributing toward a retirement fund early in their professional career and contribute regularly. This will give them the greatest chance of a sound financial retirement.
- One of the drawbacks of target-date funds is that they assume all investors have the same risk profile. Investors fall at all points along the efficient frontier, and investors that are very conservative or aggressive might not be comfortable investing in target-date funds.
- Volatility — wide, rapid swings in equity prices — is an inherent part of investing. Here are six tips to help cope with challenging markets from Principal Financial Group:
  1. Stay in the market
  2. Invest for the long-term
  3. Diversify your portfolio
  4. Consider asset allocation portfolios

> 5. Remember the benefits of long-term investing
> 6. Stay in touch with your financial professional

Bonds

Bonds are written by the government or individual companies to help raise money and are essentially IOUs. Unlike stocks, they have specific start and end dates, and when your bond matures, you will receive your investment back. Bonds come in three different lengths of time:

- Long-term bonds mature in 20 to 30 years

- Medium-term bonds mature in five to ten years

- Short-term bonds mature in one to three years

The benefit to holding a bond is being able to set a schedule for maturity. If you know you will need money at a certain time — for example, if your son or daughter will be entering college in ten years — you can get a bond that matures in ten years to ensure the money is available when you need it. Bonds are also helpful in diversifying your portfolio and in helping your portfolio endure the ups and downs of the stock market.

There are four main types of bonds: U.S. government securities, corporate bonds, municipal bonds, and zero-coupon bonds. U.S. government securities are the safest because they are issued by the federal government and, therefore, are backed by the government, meaning there is a higher likelihood you will be repaid your money when it comes due. Yet, because there is less risk involved, the return on your investment is also lower. Treasury bonds are another form of government bonds that will normally mature in ten to 30 years; you can also purchase a Treasury note that will mature more quickly, normally in two to ten years.

Corporate bonds are backed by a company and come with a higher risk because that company can default on the bond for a number of reasons. Many corporate bonds also include a stipulation through which the company can redeem the bond before it reaches full maturity, meaning you will not receive its total worth. Companies may also offer junk bonds, often called high-yield bonds, which offer a high return on investment, but are extremely risky.

Municipal bonds are issued by local government entities, such as states or cities. Many municipal bonds include the same stipulation as corporate bonds, allowing them to redeem the bond before full maturity. Do not be influenced by what you hear about municipal bonds — many times, governments will try to sell these bonds by informing you that the bond interest will be tax-deferred. If you have a 401(k) plan, this is not a benefit for you because the interest already grows tax-deferred.

The fourth type of bond, the zero-coupon bond, is commonly sold for significantly less than its mature value. These are risky, but you do not need to pay interest on the bond until it reaches full maturity.

Things to Remember

When you purchase a corporate bond, there is a chance that the company can go under, thereby lowering or wiping out what you get back in the end. Unless you are taking a high-risk gamble, buy bonds from large, reputable corporations. Of course, today, even large companies can find themselves in trouble.

By and large, there is little point to putting any tax-free or tax-deferred investment into your 401(k) account because you are already tax-sheltered. Also, because your withdrawals will be taxed, you lose the benefit of any tax-free bonds.

Chapter 5 Summary

- You can invest in mutual funds, which are a collection of stocks, bonds, and other investments purchased by a company you choose to invest some of your 401(k) account funds in.

- There are bond funds, money market funds, and stock funds available.

- Bond funds have a higher risk because the Securities and Exchange Commission does not place any restrictions on what can and cannot be invested in.

- The stock fund has the highest risk because the stock market can be volatile.

- Target-date funds are a newer option that is increasing in popularity. The target-date fund allows you to choose how many years until your retirement, and then the company holding the fund automatically reallocates your money as you age to be sure that you have less risk as you grow closer to retirement.

- You can invest in long-, medium-, or short-term bonds, and there are multiple options for purchasing them. Those from the government are the cheapest but also have the lowest rate of return. Those from individual companies are riskier because there is a chance the company can go under before it is time for them to pay you back.

- International stock funds invest outside of the United States, but because global markets do not necessarily follow U.S. trends, holding international stock can come in handy if the U.S. market takes a downturn.

- International stocks are a little riskier than U.S. stocks, but they can help to diversify your portfolio and can have good returns on investment.

- International funds are also available for you to invest in, mainly through stocks. They add more diversification to your retirement account because foreign markets do not often move exactly in sync with U.S. markets. However, there is a higher risk here, though, especially depending on what part of the world you invest in. There is also much to be gained.

6

Other Investment Options

In this chapter, you will learn:

- Why annuities can be a safe option in retirement
- About Guaranteed Investment contracts

Annuities

Another possibility for investment is an annuity, which is normally for someone looking for a certain amount of security in retirement who does not believe he or she can get it solely from a 401(k) plan. When you sign up for your retirement plan, be sure to ask your employer if he or she offers an annuity, as some employers choose to pay out employee retirement plans in this fashion. Annuities can be purchased from multiple financial institutions, but commonly come from life insurance companies. When choosing an insurance company to buy an annuity from, do as much research as possible and choose wisely — whatever company you pick will hold on to your money until you begin receiving payments. If you purchase an annuity early, you may not receive a payment for many years, so you want the insurance company to still be in business when you retire.

There are many types of annuities to choose from: immediate, deferred, fixed, variable, one that is purchased in installments, or one that is paid for up front. An immediate annuity will begin monthly payments to you up to a year after you make your purchase, while a deferred annuity will begin paying you at a time you specify at the purchase date. Fixed and variable deal with the rate of return you will receive on your investment in the annuity. A fixed annuity has a guarantee period, during which time whatever amount you have invested in the annuity will gain a fixed rate of return. This can be a good choice in an unstable economy, but there are a few things you need to think about before purchasing this type. To start, consider the current interest rate, how long it is predicted to stay there, and what it may become. Compare these numbers to your annuity contract's minimum interest rate. You should think about any fees you will have to pay on this type of account, and always be sure to ask whether you can take any money out of the account before beginning your regular withdrawals.

A variable annuity, on the other hand, has a return based on subaccounts that you choose to invest your annuity in, much like mutual funds. These are more popular than fixed annuities, but you are responsible for the risk involved in what you make because you are responsible for choosing the subaccounts. If you are only investing for a short amount of time, a variable annuity is not for you. Returns will fluctuate, so it is important to be in it for the long run to receive a decent return. Some variable annuities have extras installed in them to lure you into purchasing one. These extras may include safety against market drops, withdrawals to cover long-term care, and bonuses, which come as a percentage added to your initial annuity contribution.

Other than these choices, annuities follow basic rules. The income grows tax-deferred, and there is a 10-percent penalty on any early withdrawals, just like in a 401(k) plan. Contributions are not tax-deductible, so this is a good investment for anyone who has maxed out their contributions to a 401(k) or other retirement plan, and not a good investment choice for someone to make within a 401(k) plan. The annuity has no contribution limits or required start date for distributions, though some states require you to begin taking money out of the account by the time you turn 85. Upon your death, any payments left in your annuity will immediately roll over to your beneficiary. Should you decide that you are not getting a good rate of return on your annuity, you can switch between annuities with no penalty, known as a 1035 exchange.

Should you hold an annuity when you retire, you will receive a specified amount each month for the rest of your life, or the life of your beneficiary, if you die before the annuity runs out. Distributions are based on how old you are when you start taking them and on your life expectancy at the time. So, the older you are when you begin withdrawing funds, the more you will receive with each payment. It is important that you take money out of the annuity at some point before your death so that your beneficiaries are not stuck with high income and, if you qualify, estate taxes.

Annuities are not for everyone. If you are not currently contributing the maximum to your 401(k) or other retirement plan, do not purchase an annuity — there are high fees associated with this type of account. While both traditional retirement accounts, such as 401(k)s, IRAs, and annuities, offer tax-deferred savings, you will be losing out on the benefit of lower fees. If you only plan to save for a short time, an annuity will not benefit you, because there are penalties for those who choose to withdraw early, just like in a normal retirement savings account. Someone contributing the maximum allowed amount to another retirement savings account who does not plan to make early withdrawals or anyone who can take advantage of the tax deferral in at least the 25 percent tax bracket can benefit from an annuity.

Fast Fact

Many academics and retirees are beginning to consider annuities as the best option in retirement.

Guaranteed Investment Contracts

A Guaranteed Investment Contract (GIC) can be thought of much like a certificate of deposit that has a set interest rate during a specific length of time. GICs are issued by insurance companies and are considered safe, stable investment choices. GICs used to be popular, but the current investment attitude is geared more toward higher returns, something GICs cannot offer, especially coupled with their high fees. So, if you are looking for a higher return, stocks and bonds are the better options. It is, by and large, difficult to earn enough to surpass inflation with a GIC, meaning you will not end up with as much as you may have expected in the end. Whatever amount of your 401(k) or other retirement plan you invest in a GIC will be repaid, along with the interest accrued, when your investment term comes to an end.

GICs can be risky because unlike CDs, they are not insured by the FDIC. The only guarantee you have for receiving your money at the end of the term is based on the rating of the insurance company. So, much like choosing an annuity, it is important to do your research and choose wisely. The worse the rating of the company you choose, the less likely you are to get your money when your term ends. Insurance companies are rated by multiple firms, including Standard & Poor's, Moody's, and Fitch. The ratings vary but are based on a basic alphabetical system that ranges from AAA to D, where AAA is the highest-quality insurance company possible, and D means default — a company you want to stay away from because they have not repaid investors in the past and have not cleaned up their act.

Fast Fact
The insurance company you choose invests your money by putting it in multiple funds, including mortgages and bonds.

Chapter 6 Summary

- Annuities are a good investment if you want a steady stream of income during retirement and do not feel confident enough to make withdrawals from your 401(k) or other retirement plan yourself.

- GICs come from an insurance company and promise that you will get a set interest rate plus your initial investment back after a certain period.

- GICs are not insured by the FDIC, so it is a good idea to ensure that the insurance company you choose to buy your GIC from is reputable and expected to remain stable for a long time.

- GICs have low risk and, therefore, have a low rate of return.

- Annuities are purchased through insurance companies, so choose yours wisely, especially if you have a while before you plan to retire — you do not want the company to go under before you receive all your payments.

- GICs are like CDs and, therefore, have little risk (they are not insured by the FDIC, though, so there is a little more risk involved).

7 *Taking Risks*

In this chapter, you will learn:

- How to properly diversify a retirement account and budget for risk

- What types of risks are out there and how they can affect you

- How to recover from a loss

- What your investments are worth

- Why reallocation is vitally important to growing your nest egg

How much risk you can take is dependent on your age and planned retirement date. The younger you are, the more risk you can handle because your investments will have more time to rebound and even out when there is a downturn in the economy. But do not bail out of your high-risk investments too early — the market runs in cycles, and if you plan to make any money, you need to stay for the long run to allow your investments to even out. As you get closer to retirement, you need to begin moving into lower-risk investments where your money will have minimal return, but you will be almost certain not to lose any of your investment.

Not taking any form of risk can be a risk itself. You want to diversify your portfolio to include a multitude of risk levels to help cushion you against losing too much money in your investments. Bear in mind that no investment plan is ever guaranteed from loss unless you plan to invest all your savings in a bank account. The key is to be risky enough to make money but safe enough not to lose it all again. When you decide how much risk you can tolerate, you need to consider what you already have saved, how many years until you will retire, how long you will be retired for (and if you will have any additional income at that time), and what your current investments are returning. Never guess about what you can and cannot risk. Look at the numbers, do the math, and figure it out.

You can be too aggressive, no matter your age. When you are young and you are willing to leave your retirement money invested for a long time, it is good to have high-risk investments to allow all the ups and downs of the market to even out by the time you retire. Mentally, you can hurt yourself with too much risk. As you begin to see the market dip, your first thought may be to jump ship and sell low, even though you did not think you would feel this way; this is the worst thing you could possibly do for your investments. It is necessary to remember that losses can be hard to recover from, but normally, the longer you are invested, the better your chance to recoup any loss and make gains. If you have too much risk when you close in on your retirement date, and the market takes a significant dip, you can suffer huge losses — in tens or even hundreds of thousands of dollars. Also, at this point in life, there are not many options available to you to recover what you have lost. You will most likely need to remain in the job force or risk living retirement in poverty.

You can also be too conservative. Pessimism is normal when it comes to the economy, but do not let this drive your retirement plan. If you do not put any of your 401(k) savings into higher-risk investments, such as stocks, you do not have much growth potential, meaning you may not reach your retirement goal or may have to lower your expectations of being able to retire rich. When you near retirement, you cannot be in high-risk investments.

Diversification

Diversification can help you even out your risk. Diversification essentially means spreading your 401(k) or other retirement account dollars around to different types of investments — for example stocks, bonds, and cash, which are the three major asset classes. Diversification can protect you if one of your funds has a poor performing year. If you put all your money into one type of investment — stocks for example — every time the market takes a dip, your investment returns will drop significantly.

When deciding what to invest your retirement account funds in, you will want to ensure that the securities you choose perform at different rates — you do not want to have all your money invested in different places that all tend to track each other and perform the same at the same time. Stocks and bonds are a good example of diversification because when bond prices rise, stock prices fall.

Within each asset class or type of investment you choose, you will want to spread your money out. In stocks, you do not want all your money in one company because putting all your money into one investment can be detrimental when even the best-performing stocks hit a rough patch. Not only do you want to choose different companies if you are investing in separate stocks or holding mutual funds that invest in multiple stocks, you also want to consider the sectors that each company is in. For example, you do not want to invest in two technology companies because they will react the same way to market ups and downs. What you want to do is choose, for example, one technology stock and one oil or automotive stock. If you are investing in stocks, you want to choose large, medium, and small stocks, as well as foreign and domestic stocks. Again, in stocks or mutual funds, consider the style of each stock. For example, you should have both growth and value stocks because they represent vastly different returns. Growth stocks tend to fall fast if the stock market drops, while underpriced value stocks often have nowhere to go but up.

A Tip from Vanguard: Hypothetical Allocations

Age 20-39. Hypothetical allocation: 80 percent stocks, 20 percent bonds. For more risk-averse investors, it would be 60 percent stocks, 40 percent bonds. For less risk-averse investors, it would be 100 percent stocks.

Age 40-49. Hypothetical allocation: 60 percent stocks, 40 percent bonds. For more risk-averse investors, it would be 50 percent stocks, 50 percent bonds. For less risk-averse investors, it would be 80 percent stocks, 20 percent bonds.

Age 50-59. Hypothetical allocation: 50 percent stocks, 50 percent bonds. For more risk-averse investors, it would be 40 percent stocks, 60 percent bonds. For less risk-averse investors, it would be 60 percent stocks, 40 percent bonds.

Age 60+. Hypothetical allocation: 40 percent stocks, 60 percent bonds. For more risk-averse investors, it would be 20 percent stocks, 80 percent bonds. For less risk-averse investors, it would be 50 percent stocks, 50 percent bonds.

Investment diversification will never eliminate your risk of loss, of course, nor will it guarantee a profit in a declining market. But owning a portfolio with exposure to all key market components should give you at least some participation in whatever sectors are performing best at a given time.

Types of Risk

There are many different types of risk involved in investing, but you should not let that scare you away.

Market Risk

Market risk refers to the ups and downs of the markets you are investing in, be they stocks or otherwise. There is more risk here for the short-term investor because if you have to sell low sometimes, it can lead to big losses. Risk is lessened the more time you invest. Even though they are more risky, stocks have historically outperformed other investments.

Industry Risk

Depending on what is going on in the country and in the world at any given time, your investments may be affected. Certain industries perform better or worse depending on world events. For example, during a war, the aerospace companies will normally have increasingly valuable stock. On the other hand, some stocks are cyclical and follow the economy, and others do not. Mutual funds protect themselves from risk by spreading money across many different industries, but some invest only in specific sectors, so you need to watch out for this and protect yourself.

Business Risk

Business risk commonly only affects those who invest in a specific company rather than the market as a whole. Getting a mutual fund or investing in many different stocks can help you avoid this.

Inflation Risk

Inflation risk — the biggest risk to retirees — means that the money you invest in your retirement account today will not be worth the same when you retire: Actually, it will be worth much less because inflation eats away at the value of the dollar. If your investments return less than the rate of inflation, you will not have a good nest egg built up by the time you plan to retire. Make sure your investments are keeping pace with or exceeding the inflation rate, which is, by and large, about 3 to 5 percent per year, but it can be much higher. If your investments are consistently returning less than inflation, you may need to seek help from a professional investor to create a projected plan that will take into account the rising rate of inflation.

Interest Rate Risk

The interest rate will mostly affect the different bond values. Characteristically, when interest rates go up, bond prices go down. The same thing happens to the stock market — when the market's value drops because interest rates go up, the stocks begin competing heavily with bonds.

Credit Risk

Again, credit risk will affect the bond market more than the stock market. The risk here is that the government entity or business that sold you the bond will default on it, and you will not receive the full value of the bond. U.S. government bonds are the safest to hold, while high-yield bonds are the riskiest but have the best rate of return if the company does not default. Be sure to look at the ratings of the companies issuing you the bond, which you can get from Moody's or S&P.

Preparing for and Recovering from a Loss

Unless you invest solely in cash funds, you do stand to lose money in your investments, but you will normally recoup them over time, as long as you stay focused on your long-term goal and do not get out of the market quickly when the economy takes a downturn. If, after your first loss, you decide that you can no longer stomach how much your investment balance dropped, when the market evens back out, consider changing your investment ratio — perhaps you were not as risky as you thought you were.

A Tip from Vanguard

Market downturns are inevitable; so are market recoveries. Before changing anything, take a moment to reflect on you portfolio and the process that you used to create it.

First, do you have a well-thought-out strategy? Many investors choose funds based on their performance instead of choosing funds based on the diversification they will provide to their portfolio. Asset allocation and diversification are investors' most readily available means for moderating the risks inherent in investing.

Second, investors should always look to see whether they are truly diversified. Investors may have a number of funds (too many, in many cases), yet those funds may often use similar strategies or invest in too-similar companies. As a result, their portfolios are less diversified than they think.

Finally, investors should revisit their risk tolerance. When market returns are positive, people often overestimate their ability to withstand market declines. This is much more common than investors might want to admit, and research into behavioral finance notes that investors tend to be loss-averse — that is, investors dislike losses more significantly than they like gains. And, while the stock market has historically delivered positive returns most years, when it does not, those losses can be severe. Author Peter Bernstein noted that "consequences matter more than probabilities," and investors tend to keep that notion foremost in their minds when planning their portfolio.

In the end, for investors who have built a sound investment strategy and a well-diversified portfolio, staying the course is probably the best course of action. For those who have not, investing time to develop their strategy is probably the most rewarding step that they can take.

Figuring Out What Your Investments Are Worth

If you want to know how many years it will take for you to double your investment, there is a simple formula known as the Rule of 72. Figure out the annual return on your investments. Then divide 72 by this number to find out how many years until you double your money. For example, if you have a 10 percent annual return, 72/.10 is 7.2, meaning it will take you 7.2 years to double your money; a 5 percent annual return will take 14.4 years to double your money.

Your annual return on your investments is how much your initial investment has grown or not grown over time. It is made up of interest or dividends paid and change in the value of your investment (stock and bond, for example). The total is commonly figured annually as a percentage.

Reallocation

When it comes to investing, an important concept is how you will reallocate your investment mix. As previously stressed, it is important to be checking in on your 401(k) or other retirement account to ensure that you are comfortable with your level of risk and are earning what you expected from the start. While it would be unwise to reallocate or move your 401(k) account funds around from investment to investment all the time, you need to check in and reallocate as you age, as your lifestyle changes or as your investments perform better or worse than you had originally expected. There are different ways to rebalance your account. As you strive to achieve the perfect balance, you can move your investments around, switching between stocks and bonds, international and domestic funds, and corporate and government funds, for example. Or, you can leave your money in the funds it is already in and simply change what you put into each investment in the future

A Tip from Vanguard

To make it easy to remember, time your rebalancing to coincide with a memorable date, such as a birthday or anniversary. Then, to restore your asset allocation to its target, you have several options:

- Add new money to the asset class that has fallen below its target percentage

- Direct dividend and capital gains distributions from the asset class that exceeds its target into the underweighted class

- Exchange money from the highest-returning asset class (noting that there may be tax consequences when you exchange between taxable accounts)

You will certainly want to keep a hard copy of what types of investments you hold, what amount of your 401(k) account you have invested in it, and what percentage of your 401(k) account that investment makes up. To figure out what percentage of your 401(k) account you have in a certain investment, you simply divide the amount you have in a certain investment (bonds, for example) by the total amount you have in your 401(k) account.

A Tip from Vanguard

Rebalancing may result in taking some money away from the top performer of the moment. While that can be emotionally difficult, such investment discipline will help prevent you from becoming too heavily weighted in one area. Diversification is a fundamental best investment practice, and rebalancing can be a way to make sure you achieve or maintain diversification. Investors, of course, want to buy low and sell high, and that is what rebalancing can help you do.

There are a few different things you need to look out for when deciding on the best time to rebalance. If you have investments that are far outperforming other investments in your account, you may want to consider putting any new dollars you decide to invest toward the underperforming investments because they have nowhere to go but up, while the stocks that are performing extremely well have a better chance of dropping off sooner. Bear in mind that past performance does not ever indicate future performance. As odd as it may sound, you also want to reallocate your expectations. As you rebalance your account, be sure to look at your original retirement plan and determine whether you are on track to meet that goal and should leave your investments where they are, whether you can consider less risk, or need to invest in higher-risk (and higher-return) investments.

A Tip from ShareBuilder

Typically, a downturn is a great time to buy. Often, people panic during downturns and shift their monies to what they think is a better-performing area. Then, when they see the fund area they left a year or two ago recover with good results, they shift back and miss most, if not all, the return they would have received if they had stuck with their plan. Always look before you leap. Just keep in mind your investment horizon and your asset allocation that matches your goals (mix between stocks, bonds, and cash), and you will tend to be better off than those who make decisions fueled by hot topics of the day and short-term speculation.

A Tip from ShareBuilder

Checking in and rebalancing your stock, bonds, and cash mix helps you stay on track to meet your goals. Often, one asset class will outperform another over a given year and will over-weight your risk. Stick with your plan and the asset allocation you have chosen. Even if one fund is hot now, it will not be forever. By rebalancing, you help manage that risk and keep your savings plan on course.

Fast Fact

According to *When the Good Pensions Go Away* by Thomas J. Mackell Jr., 90 percent of Americans who choose how to allocate their investments and make specific investment choices never change them.

Managing Your 401(k) Account While You Remain in the Job Force

It would be unwise of you to assume that you can let your 401(k) account investments run themselves until you retire and decide that you need to begin making withdrawals. You should always be aware of what your investments are doing and how they are affecting your retirement outlook. Find out whether you have online access to any of your 401(k) investments or to your 401(k) account in broad. If you are able to access it online, you may be able to reallocate your investments on the Web rather than having to go to anyone within your plan. The more control you have or can assert, the better off you will be. After you have chosen your actual asset allocation — where your 401(k) or other retirement account funds are invested — you need to create benchmarks for your account that you can follow from day to day, month to month, or whatever you chose your time period to be. By and large, a benchmark means knowing from day to day how your stocks are doing, which you can follow in most major, or even local, newspapers. *The Wall Street Journal* is a particularly good place to look for stock performance. Your benchmark could also be an index — or average of the entire stock market — or a particular sector that you invest in. Once you have set your benchmark, you need to know when it is time to rebalance or reallocate your investments.

Chapter 7 Summary

- You can be too risky or too conservative.

- The younger you are, the more risk you can handle.

- As you get older, you want to move into lower-risk investments to ensure that a dip in the market does not affect any retirement funds you are planning to take in the near future — if there is a big drop, and you are invested in risky funds, you will not have time to recover, and this may ruin your retirement plans.

- There are multiple types of risk, including business risk, credit risk, market risk, inflation risk, interest rate risk, and industry risk.

8 *Changing Employers*

In this chapter, you will learn:

- What to do with your 401(k) or other retirement account when you change employers

There is no need to worry about losing your 401(k) funds if you change jobs — even if you do so often. The amount in your 401(k) account when you leave your employer may dictate where your money is required to go. If you have more than $5,000 in the account, you cannot leave the money in your old employer's plan. If you have between $1,000 and $5,000 dollars, your employer may be able to make the decision to put this money in an IRA automatically, based on the stipulations laid out in your summary plan description. Finally, if you have less than $1,000 in the account, most employers will require that you withdraw this money in one lump sum.

If you want to avoid paying taxes, you can either roll over your 401(k) money into an IRA or into your new employer's plan. Should you choose to put your money into an IRA, you can do a partial or complete rollover. Once the money is in the IRA, you will not be able to take out loans against yourself, but you will be able to withdraw money at anytime — though there will be penalties, unless you are making a withdrawal for your primary residence or higher education. In most cases, the best decision to make when you change employers is to roll your current retirement account funds into an IRA because you will have an easier time picking which investments you would like to reinvest in.

Choosing to move your money to your new employer's plan is a good idea if the new plan is better than an IRA, you want a significant amount of convenience, or you plan on needing a loan in the near future. Be sure to pay attention to the rules on both ends to ensure you are able to do a rollover and also to ensure there are no stipulations that prevent you from accessing your money. You do not have to roll over to another 401(k) plan. If your new employer offers a 457 or 403(b) plan, you can roll over into one of those as well; see Chapter 13 for more information on these types of plans.

If you decide to put your current 401(k) account into an IRA, be sure that your employer deposits the money directly into the new account and does not hand you a check for the amount currently in your 401(k). If you are given a check, 20 percent will be taken out as taxes, and you will be required to pay that 20 percent back to the account you roll over into the IRA — and you will only have 60 days to come up with all the money and make the transfer. If even a penny of the check your employer gave you goes missing, you will be subject to income taxes on the missing portion and early withdrawal fees.

If you hold company stock when you leave your current job or retire, there are specific rules you need to follow to reap the tax savings. A special rule, known as net unrealized appreciation, allows you to move employer stock from your 401(k) account when you leave the company. To pay a lower tax rate on the company stock, you have to take a lump-sum withdrawal of the entire amount in your 401(k) account. After making the withdrawal, all of the money — except the company stock — must be put into an IRA, while any company stock must go into a taxable account, such as a normal bank savings account. The stock will be penalized 10 percent if you are younger than 59 and a half, and you will have to pay income taxes, but you will be taxed at the price you bought the stock at rather than its market price. You will not be taxed on the money in the IRA until you begin making withdrawals.

Another option is to leave your money where it is: in your old employer's plan. This is an option if you are feeling lazy or your new employer does not offer a retirement savings plan. Always choose a 401(k) over an IRA because you are better protected during personal and corporate bankruptcy. Your old employer may be able to make changes to your account regarding types of investments you are able to make: You will have little support if you have a problem, you will not be able to take loans against yourself, and you will not be able to make any additional contributions, but you will still be able to rebalance your account to ensure your investments are growing at a rate you would like.

Your final option is to withdraw the money from the account. Should you choose to do this, you will be taxed and penalized, unless you are over age 55, in which case, there will be no penalty charged to you. This is because the government believes that if you leave your employer at age 55, you are unlikely to find a new job before turning 59 and a half, when you are able to make penalty-free withdrawals anyway. Commonly, taking one large withdrawal is a bad idea in the end, as your account will not have the potential to grow as much before you retire. According to a 2005 study conducted by Hewitt Associates, approximately half of all workers withdrew all the money from their 401(k) plan when they left an employer, sacrificing future tax-deferred growth.

In most cases, the best decision to make when you change employers is to roll your current retirement account funds into an IRA or your new employer's 401(k) rather than leaving the funds with your old employer because you will have an easier time picking which investments you would like to reinvest in.

If you decide to leave your current employer for a new one, ensure that you are fully vested and will receive all your employer's contributions to your 401(k) account. If you still have some time before your employer's funds are considered 100 percent yours, weigh your options — you do not want to give up free money, so think about whether staying with your current employer for a couple more years is an option. Or, if you will have a higher salary — and, therefore, more money to put into your retirement savings account — you may be better off leaving your current job without being fully vested.

Even if you are hired at a new job that you do not plan to stay with for an extended time, do not let that stop you from opening a 401(k) account. Do not forget that it can move from job to job with you, so you should not miss out on even a few months' worth of contributions.

Chapter 8 Summary

- Deciding to leave your employer can be difficult, but deciding what to do with your 401(k) account can be even more stressful.

- When you leave your employer, you have the option of taking all the money out of your 401(k) account, rolling it over into your new employer's retirement account, opening up an IRA and rolling the money into it, or leaving your money where it is.

- If you can avoid it, never accept a check made out to you for the balance in your old 401(k) — arrange for a direct transfer of money. If the money is not directly transferred, you will be responsible for moving the money, and you could owe penalties and income taxes, especially if you do not complete the rollover within 60 days.

- Be sure to check your vesting status before you leave your employer because you want to be fully invested before you leave or at least close enough that you feel comfortable leaving behind free money. You do not need to worry about what will happen to your retirement funds if you change jobs — you can take the money in the account with you, roll it over into your new employer's account, roll it into an IRA, or withdraw the money in a lump sum.

9 Withdrawing Funds

In this chapter, you will learn:

- How to withdraw funds when you are at your normal retirement age

- The options for early withdrawals

- Why early withdrawals can hurt your retirement

- What your beneficiaries should know and do in the event of your death

No matter what, someone — be it you or your beneficiaries — will have to withdraw funds from your 401(k) account. The question is when, how, and how much trouble will it be when you do so. The federally approved retirement age is 65, but you are able to draw money out of your account before that time, both with and without penalty.

When you consider your withdrawal amounts, consider how much you will have to pay in taxes, because if you can only afford to pay out a certain amount each year in taxes, you do not want to bankrupt yourself just to take a few extra dollars out of your retirement account. Besides, there is also compounding interest to consider.

Early Withdrawals

Early withdrawals can put a huge dent in your retirement savings and be the difference between a sports car and a station wagon, but they are necessary to mention in this book. To make any type of early withdrawal, you must have an "immediate and heavy financial need," according to the IRS.

Many employers will allow you to withdraw from your 401(k) account before retirement, but you must have a valid reason. One reason is known as hardship. The hardship withdrawal is for people who are having financial difficulties. If you absolutely need to make a hardship withdrawal, you must prove that you have no other means of covering your bills.

If you do not have enough information to prove you need a hardship withdrawal, or if you are uncomfortable with all the invasive questions, another option is the deemed hardship withdrawal. There is not as much information involved in this type of withdrawal, so it is not as invasive. However, you must be able to meet one of the IRS's valid reasons. This list includes the purchase of your primary residence, paying college or other post-secondary education bills for yourself or your dependents, health care, and costs involved in preventing eviction and foreclosure on your primary residence.

Bear in mind that you must pay taxes on any form of hardship withdrawal, so it would be wise to add up the amount you will owe in taxes and the amount you plan to withdraw — which will be capped at how much you need to cover your bills — so that you can withdraw the entire amount. Another important point to note is that many times, there is a six-month waiting period applied to your 401(k) account before you are able to begin contributing again if you take an early withdrawal. After this wait period, you will be capped on how much you are able to contribute to your account. To figure out what you can contribute, subtract what you contributed the year before you took your withdrawal from the federal maximum. For example, if you contributed $5,500 the year before your withdrawal, and the federal maximum is $15,500, after the waiting period, you will be able to contribute $10,000 per year.

No matter what type of early withdrawal you decide to take, you may not be able to withdraw any of your employer's contributions, even if the contributions are fully vested.

Another type of early withdrawal is the loan. Some employers may require that you take out a loan against yourself before making any hardship withdrawal. As with hardship withdrawals, you must have a good reason for taking the loan, and it must fall under one of the IRS's approved reasons. Should you decide to take a loan, do not forget that you will need to pay it back to yourself, with interest. Yet, instead of writing checks to yourself or your 401(k) account, you will repay the loan through a pre-tax paycheck deduction. Also, take note that if you take a loan, you will be double-taxed — once for interest while you have the loan out and once again when you retire and begin making withdrawals.

Warning: Do not take a loan if you cannot pay it back while continuing to make contributions to your 401(k) plan. Always focus on making contributions first. There are many downsides to taking out a loan against yourself. You will have to repay yourself with interest, and you will have to pay yourself back immediately. One advantage to taking out a loan against yourself is that you will get a better interest rate than you most likely would if you went straight to the bank for a loan. You will also be able to get money faster from your own 401(k) account than from a bank.

If you become disabled before retirement, or have medical expenses equal to or more than 7.5 percent of your income, you can avoid withdrawal penalties by taking a Substantially Equal Periodic Payments (SEPP)/72(t) Payments withdrawal. SEPP requires you to set up a five-year payment schedule (or until you are 59 and a half — whichever is longer). In the case of disability, you must be able to prove that you will not be able to work again. At this time, your employer contributions are normally considered fully vested. You cannot change your payments until your payment schedule period is over. If you decide to withdraw more at some point before your schedule is over, you will be forced to pay a penalty on the current and previous withdrawals you made, plus interest, which will all be due in the year that you make the adjustment.

When you take a loan from yourself, you need to figure out what your interest rate will be. Your employer will be in charge of choosing the interest rate based on IRS standards, and it is often the prime rate plus a few percentage points. Most often, the interest that you have to pay on the loan will go back into your retirement account. Your 401(k) plan does not have to allow you to take out a loan. If they do allow it, the loan must be secure, and your interest rate must be reasonable — the amount is limited to 50 percent of your account balance or $50,000, whichever is less, and must be repaid in five years (or 15 years if it is a residential loan).

Be sure to find out whether your plan can prohibit you from making any withdrawals before you reach age 65, even if you are leaving your employer or if you have retired before that point.

CASE STUDY: ANALYSIS OF THE ECONOMICS OF EARLY SOCIAL SECURITY WITHDRAWAL

By Robert J. Phillips
Chief Retirement Consultant for
www.retirementcalc.com
Used with permission:
www.retirementcalc.com

Deciding whether to take the early withdrawal of social security at age 62 can be difficult. If you need this income at 62 to fund your retirement, the decision is fairly straightforward — take it early. On the other hand, if you have another source of revenue to fund your retirement, your decision will be primarily based on lifestyle, health, and investment preferences.

Several factors can affect your decision. First is your life expectancy. If you are in good health, and have a family history of living beyond 90, then waiting for full benefits may be best. Two other factors impact this decision. First and most important is the value of money or your expected return from your investments. If you are using other investments instead of social security to fund your retirement, you should use the rate of return of these investments as your value of money. There is another way to look at the value of money. If you do not require the social security money to live, you can invest the distributions for the future. The rate of return of this investment is your value of money. If you have investments that will make larger returns, such as stocks, this would favor taking the early withdrawal.

The last factor impacting your decision is inflation. Social security includes an annual adjustment based on inflation. You cannot control this variable, but you should be aware of its impact. If future inflation is significant, it will favor a later full distribution.

CASE STUDY: ANALYSIS OF THE ECONOMICS OF EARLY SOCIAL SECURITY WITHDRAWAL

We developed a calculator to assist in analyzing the impact of taking early benefits at age 62 or waiting for full benefits at age 66 to 67, depending on the year you were born. If you were born in 1960 or later, your full benefits will begin at age 67 and your reduction for early benefits at age 62 will be 30 percent. If you were born between 1946 and 1960, your full benefits begin as early as age 66. We have included a chart that summarizes information.

Year of Birth	Full (normal) Retirement Age	At age 65, the retirement benefit is reduced by:
1937 or earlier	65	20 percent
1938	65 and two months	20.83 percent
1939	65 and four months	21.67 percent
1940	65 and six months	22.50 percent
1941	65 and eight months	23.33 percent
1942	65 and ten months	24.17 percent
1943 to 1954	66	25 percent
1955	66 and two months	25.83 percent
1956	66 and four months	26.67 percent
1957	66 and six months	27.50 percent
1958	66 and eight months	28.33 percent
1959	66 and ten months	29.17 percent
1960 and later	67	30 percent
*Chart from the Social Security Administration, Retirement Planner, www.socialsecurity.gov		

To use the calculator, you need to input your year of birth. You also need to input a value of money up to 10 percent and a projected inflation adjustment. The calculator analyzes income generated over time from both the early and full benefit investments. It calculates the age at which full social security will catch up and break even with the early withdrawal. If you were born before 1960, your break even age will be impacted by the year you were born. An early break even age favors waiting for full benefits.

CASE STUDY: ANALYSIS OF THE ECONOMICS OF EARLY SOCIAL SECURITY WITHDRAWAL

The social security calculator is not the final answer on whether to take an early withdrawal, but it does give you additional economic data to assist in that decision. Ultimately, you must balance income, investments, and lifestyle to optimize your enjoyment during your retirement years.

Fast Fact

According to Transamerica, in 2007, one out of every five people with a retirement plan took a loan out, up from one in ten in 2006.

Action Item

You should not see your retirement account as a bank or a place where you can take a loan whenever you need it. This should not be your fallback plan — you need to have an emergency savings fund for these problems or at least begin living closer to your means while working.

Fast Fact

A CNN poll from February 20, 2008, shows that 54 percent of people use their 401(k) accounts to pay for monthly expenses.

Fast Fact

USA Today reports that people are using their 401(k) plans to stop the bank from foreclosing on them.

Normal Retirement Withdrawals

When you reach age 59 and a half, you can begin taking money out of your 401(k) account penalty-free, as long as your employer allows it. Some employers stipulate in the summary plan description that you must wait until

65 (for someone born before 1938) or 67 (for someone born after 1959) to begin withdrawing funds. Deciding how much to withdraw, when to withdraw it, and how to continue helping your 401(k) account grow can be more difficult than making investment choices while you are in the workforce. Each person has different needs, so, unfortunately, there is no one plan that will suit everyone.

One model that some people choose to use is known as the 4 percent solution, which says that you should take 4 percent out of your retirement account during your first year in retirement and increase that amount each year to keep up with inflation. This is an exceptionally conservative method, but if you fear running out of money before retirement, the 4 percent solution almost guarantees that you will be able to make steady withdrawals throughout your entire retirement. Or, if you would rather have a steady stream of income driven by someone else, you can purchase an immediate annuity, through which an insurance company will send you monthly payments for the rest of your life. You can choose how much you want to give to the insurance company to purchase the annuity, which can be based on paying certain monthly bills, or you can hand over your entire retirement account amount and have larger payments. But if you choose to put just a portion of your 401(k) account toward an immediate annuity, you can invest the rest in more risky stocks or mutual funds and still be guaranteed enough money to pay off monthly bills. These solutions are not necessarily for everyone and will not always work to the best of your interest — be sure to do the research and figure out what is most appropriate for your current situation and your retirement plans.

In today's economy, an immediate annuity is not necessarily the best choice for making withdrawals. Because an annuity is a fixed-rate investment, the low interest rates, coupled with inflation, are significantly decreasing the buying power of things like annuities, meaning any retiree that has one now or is considering buying one in the near future will have to supplement his or her income in the future or consider cutting back on spending.

You are required to take money out of your 401(k) account once you reach age 70 and a half, even if you are still working for the employer who holds your plan, or you can be fined up to 50 percent of the amount that you were supposed to withdraw at that time. You are also required to withdraw a certain amount, known as your required minimum distribution (RMD). Your first withdrawal must be taken by April 1 the year after you turn 70 and a half. So, if you turn 70 and a half on August 1, 2040, you are required, by federal law, to make your first withdrawal by April 1, 2041. But, if you are thinking of waiting until the last minute to make that withdrawal, think again.

Every year after your first withdrawal, you must make a withdrawal by December 31. This means if you wait until April 1 to make your first withdrawal, you will have to take a second withdrawal that year before December 31. This might not seem like such a bad thing, until you consider the taxes you will be paying on interest. You do not want to pay double taxes one year. You can delay your required begin date for your required minimum distributions as long as you are still working, but you can only delay the start to age 70 and a half. If you have an IRA or one of the other plans held by a company where you were an employee, you are not able to delay your start date.

As mentioned, you are required to take a certain amount from your account each year after you reach age 70 and a half. The complicated formula used to figure this out involves your account balance and your life expectancy during the year you are taking the withdrawal. The IRS has a table that dictates life expectancy, which can be found at **www.irs.gov/pub/irs-pdf/p590.pdf**, their Publication 590. Plus, in the event that you own an IRA as well, the rules for distribution are the same.

When considering your 401(k) withdrawal options, here are some things to think about. Each withdrawal option can have its own pros and cons.

- You can leave your money in your employer's 401(k) fund and then withdraw from it later. You are, though, required to begin taking money out of the account once you reach age 70 and a half. The upside to this is that you do not need to make an immediate decision as to what to do with your money, so you will be able to stick with an account and investments that are familiar to you, rather than spending time learning about new investments. The downside to this is that your investment choices will be more limited after you retire than while you are in the job force. This may mean that you are stuck with investments you are not happy with, and then you may not get the return you are looking for. If your employer happens to go bankrupt, you could lose some of your matching funds or may experience a long wait time when you try to get the money out of your account.

- Another option is to take all the money out of your account in one lump sum. If you choose to do this, one positive aspect is that you can use this money for any use in retirement, and you will not have to wait for a check to arrive in the mail. The downside, though, is that if you spend all the money right away, you will not have any money for later in your retirement, and you will be stuck relying on your social security payments, if you are lucky enough to receive them. You will also be hit with a ton of income taxes, and you will have to pay for the entire amount up front. In addition, if you are taking the lump sum before age 59 and a half, you will have to pay a penalty. The lump-sum withdrawal option should only be considered if you have pressing financial needs, such as covering medical or housing bills, or if you have a low balance in your 401(k) account. If you need to take the money out all at once, you will not get a tax break. If you hold company stock and choose only to take that out in one lump sum, you will benefit from net unrealized appreciation and can pay your normal income tax rate on the stock cost when you bought it rather than its current value. If you were born before 1936, you are eligible for a program known as ten-year averaging (as long as you meet a list of stipulations), which means you will pay a lower income tax rate on a lump-sum distribution (based off the tax rates in 1986). But, should you just decide to take the money all at once and be in a situation where you need to pay the taxes up front, you and your beneficiaries will not have to worry about paying taxes later, though there will also not be any further appreciation of the value of your account.

- Another option is to roll the entire amount of your 401(k) account into an IRA. This can be good for you because of the flexibility an IRA offers in terms of investments — you will have the option of stocks, bonds, and mutual funds, and you can buy and sell them at any time. There is not a huge drawback to doing this, but if you are not careful and you take a check from your employer rather than having him or her roll the money directly into your IRA without it ever crossing your hands, you will have to make up the 20 percent your employer will take for taxes out of your own pocket. Also, if you do not do so within 60 days, you will be fined and forced to pay income taxes on any missing amount.

- If your employer allows, you can choose to convert your 401(k) account to an annuity, and you will benefit from receiving regular payments. Annuities are beneficial to people who do not want to have to manage an account in retirement and would rather just receive a fixed amount each year. The downside to this is that there are many forms of annuities, and they can vary widely, so you will need to do a ton of research before choosing one of the options. Be careful, because some require you to take all your payments within a certain number of years, while others will cover your life and that of a surviving dependent. If you are considering an annuity but are not yet ready to commit to when you retire, consider putting the money into an IRA and using some of your IRA money to purchase an annuity later, once you have done the appropriate research. This can benefit you because you will not be forced to put all your money into one annuity — you can choose how much goes in.

- Another option is taking the money out of your 401(k) account in installments, as long as your employer allows you to. These payments will normally need to be completed within five, ten, or 15 years. This is a good choice for you if you are planning to leave your 401(k) funds with your current employer once you retire. This is also a good choice if you need to have a stream of income coming in but are uncomfortable with buying an annuity. The downside is that you will not have much choice in your investments, which means you may be limited to investment options you are not interested in and ones that will not allow you to follow your retirement plan.

- Finally, you can choose to combine any number of these options. This is a good idea for many people who need to have a plan that most closely fits their long-term retirement plan. There is no one-size-fits-all deal here — you can choose how much to pull out or put into a certain account, meaning you can allocate money specially to a house, bills, or whatever else you may need to pay for in retirement. The downside is that you will have many accounts that you need to keep track of, and it can get incredibly confusing, involving so much maneuvering and research.

Action Item

Figure out the most tax-friendly way to withdraw your retirement funds — for both you and your beneficiaries.

Beneficiary Withdrawals

When signing up for your 401(k) plan, be sure to ask your employer (or find in your summary plan description) how your beneficiaries will receive funds from your 401(k) account in the event of your death.

Before 2008, if you had been the beneficiary of a 401(k), you were required to take a lump sum, either immediately or stretched out over a few years. Now, should you be the recipient of a 401(k) account balance from someone other than your spouse, you are able to put that money directly into an IRA — something that only spouses had been able to do before this time. This provides some beneficiaries the ability to stretch tax payments over a longer time while the investments continue to grow in the account. For anyone other than a spouse to be able to take advantage of rolling the money directly into an IRA, he or she must follow specific rules. The money must go directly into an inherited IRA — not a traditional or Roth IRA — that will be titled with the name of the deceased whose account you are receiving to your benefit. Companies, though, are not required to put the deceased owner's 401(k) account directly into an IRA that you request. If the employer gives you a check, be sure that it is made out in the name of the retirement account and not directly to you.

Things to Remember

No matter what kind of withdrawal you make, you want to consider the taxes you will have to pay. Many people do not believe that they qualify for the estate tax, but you might have to pay the estate tax, even if you think it is only for wealthy people living in large homes. The estate tax, for those who die in 2008, does not begin until your estate is valued at $2 million. That may sound like a high number, but do not underestimate what you own. You need to think about compounding interest, properties, and any retirement or other savings accounts you have. Some states have estate taxes and some do not, so be aware of what your state has. The estate tax is set to end in 2010 but is expected to be reenacted in 2011.

Chapter 9 Summary

- You can make withdrawals from your 401(k) account while you are at your current job before age 59 and a half, which is not recommended, or you can take normal retirement withdrawals when you reach full retirement age.

- If you need emergency money, you can get a loan from yourself, make a hardship withdrawal (but in both cases you will incur fees), or, in some cases, you can take money out of your 401(k) account to cover your first home and medical fees. You can withdraw money from your 401(k) or other retirement account before age 59 and a half, but you will be penalized.

- Some 401(k) plans allow you to take a loan out against yourself, but you will have to repay it.

- Hardship withdrawals will require you to meet a long list of specifications.

- Normal retirement withdrawals must be taken after age 59 and a half but before age 70 and a half.

- You have a required begin date when you must begin taking withdrawals and a required minimum distribution that you must take.

- You can take a withdrawal in one lump sum.

- You can leave your money in your employer's 401(k) and take withdrawals from there.

- You can roll your current 401(k) account into an IRA, and you can convert that to a Roth IRA for higher contribution limits.

- If your employer allows you to, you can use your 401(k) funds to purchase an annuity, which will ensure that you have monthly fixed payments until the account runs out.

- You can pull the money out of your account in installments, but it must be completed in five, ten, or 15 years.

- You can also combine a bunch of different investment and withdrawal options to form something that best fits your lifestyle.

- You will need to find out how your beneficiaries will make withdrawals — it is important that they are informed of the things to know about your account so that upon your death, they know whom to contact and how to make withdrawals.

10 *What to Expect as You Grow Closer to Your Retirement Date*

In this chapter, you will learn:

- What to do when you are close to retirement

- About social security and other benefits available to you in retirement

- How to shift your retirement account funds into less-risky options

As you inch closer to retirement, you need to start thinking about whether you will be able to stick with your original retirement age you planned on or if you are not yet ready to live off your retirement savings. If you have been investing in the plan for long enough and saving enough, you should be nearly financially ready for your retirement by this point.

If you have decided you will be able to retire, ensure your 401(k) or other retirement plan accounts are in low-risk investments. At this point, you should have no reason to gamble with high-risk investments, so it is better to keep your account stable and the money coming in, though it may seem to slow to a trickle if you spent most of your working life with high-risk, high-yield investments that were performing well.

Fast Fact

According to the Health and Retirement Study, between the 1950s and mid 1980s, more men began opting for retirement before full retirement age. Since 1990, however, the number of older men in the workforce has increased slightly. As for women, the rate at which they are still working past age 60 has increased significantly in the past two decades.

Fast Fact

According to the Health and Retirement Study, there are differences between the races in terms of retirement age. Black men are nearly 8 percent more likely to be retired than white men at age 57. In their 60s, white men are more likely to be retired than Hispanic men. Black women are more likely to work than white women, and Hispanic women are more likely to be retired than white women once they reach age 55.

This is also a good time to start thinking about when you plan to take your social security benefits. The following table lists full retirement ages and how much your social security benefits will be reduced if you decide to take your benefits earlier. Think about how much you need them, and if you can, hold out until full retirement age to begin taking them, even if you left your job and began taking withdrawals from your retirement account before full retirement age.

Many investment and retirement experts recommend that their clients choose a target retirement date, and about a year away from that date, try living off the income they have planned to have in retirement. If the future retiree finds that he or she is comfortable with that income level, he or she is ready to let the employer know that retirement is not too far off in this employee's future. If this person decides that he or she cannot possibly survive on the target retirement income, it is time to push retirement back and consider working longer or contributing more to a retirement account.

Retirement Benefits: How Much They Reduce Pending On Year of Birth*		
Year of Birth	Full (normal) Retirement Age	Retirement Benefit Reduce By
1937 or earlier	65	20%
1938	65 and 2 months	20.83%
1939	65 and 4 months	21.67%
1940	65 and 6 months	22.50%
1941	65 and 8 months	23.33%
1942	65 and 10 months	24.17%
1943-1954	66	25%
1955	66 and 2 months	25.83%
1956	66 and 4 months	26.67%
1957	66 and 6 months	27.50%
1958	66 and 8 months	28.33%
1959	66 and 10 months	29.17%
1960 or later	67	30%

* Chart from the Social Security Administration, Retirement Planner, www.socialsecurity.gov

Be sure you are aware of your company's withdrawal plan for employees at full retirement age and before. By and large, you will be able to make normal withdrawals at age 59 and a half, or if you leave your employer after age

55. Know how the money will be distributed to you and whether you have an option on how much you get with each withdrawal, how often you have to take them, and whether you need to withdraw in one lump sum. Also, find out how your beneficiary will receive your 401(k) benefits should you die before taking all the money out of your account.

If you decide you will be able to live well without beginning to withdraw money from your 401(k) account after retiring, start making plans for what you will do with your money at age 70 and a half, when you must start taking your required minimum distributions.

> ### Action Item
> Decide before you reach full retirement age whether you will begin taking your required minimum distributions then or will wait until you reach age 70 and a half.

> ### Action Item
> It is also a good idea to request a copy of your social security statement to see how much you have paid into the fund and get an estimate of how much you can expect in retirement.

It is important to consider where you will live when you retire. Different parts of the country have different costs of living for both housing and other expenses — cities have a higher cost, while if you live out in the country, your cost is likely to be lower.

When you are approximately ten years away from retirement, begin making concrete plans for what you will do when you finally retire. Will you stay in your current home? Will you continue to work? If so, will you work full-time or part-time? Do you need this money to pay your necessary bills, or will it be "fun money" to spend on cars, trips, movies, and other luxuries? Will you travel? Will you move closer to be near your children or grandchildren?

Fast Fact

With poor debt, mortgage, and housing markets, the future is looking increasingly bleak for baby boomers who are preparing to retire within the next five years. The bad news for them is that it will be difficult to turn everything around as quickly as they need it.

Fast Fact

According to the Census Bureau, the ratio of people aged 65 and older and those who are considered to be in prime working years — between the ages of 20 and 64 — will rise approximately 15 percent between 2005 and 2030.

At this point, you also need to begin contributing more, if you can afford it, to your retirement savings plan, because even if you already have enough saved, it is nice to have a safety net that you can count on to see you through any emergencies. If you have enough to make larger contributions to your retirement account and still have money left over, pay down any debts you have so that you do not need to be concerned with them in retirement.

Five years from retirement, begin figuring out how much you will make each month or year during retirement (whichever makes more sense for your purposes)—consider what you will be bringing in from retirement accounts, jobs, and other sources, and also what you have on hand. Be sure to visit your doctor to discuss any long-term care issues you may be facing — even though some may catch you by surprise, getting the doctor's opinion is definitely worth it. Think about what your retirement budget will be once you have estimated how much you will be making. What bills will you still need to pay?

Once you are a few years from retiring, look over all your investments and your social security plan to figure out exactly how much you should be receiving during retirement. Also, if you plan to move, begin visiting places you are interested in to see whether you still like them.

Action Item

Three months from your 65th birthday, sign up for Medicare benefits.

Action Item

Decide where you are going to live and whether you anticipate needing long-term care. Have a retirement budget — do not go into your retirement years blindly.

Action Item

Plan like you are going to live past 100.

Fast Fact

Fidelity Investments estimates that to cover long-term care costs, the average 65-year-old couple will need $215,000.

Action Item

Join the AARP.

Action Item

Visit your doctor to discuss any problems that may be on your horizon.

If you are planning to retire in the next few years, or if you find yourself planning to retire a few years away from a financial crisis, you need to begin looking at your finances and finding any way you can to cut corners. Anything extra you can invest will not completely make up for what you have lost in the economy, but it can make up a little bit — especially if you do not plan to continue working.

If you are an older retiree, be sure you know about federal and state laws that can help protect what you have saved for retirement and detail what happens when you file for bankruptcy — not knowing can cost you your entire savings.

Action Item

So, what do you do if you retire and need help?

- Go to a professional, nonprofit consumer counselor (be sure you are not being charged for services).

- Do not get a reverse mortgage.

- Be careful about refinancing your mortgage — make sure that you have enough to pay the new amount.

- Use your retirement dollars wisely.

- Find a lawyer if you need to file bankruptcy or feel you are being taken advantage of by investment companies or credit card companies, for example.

Action Item

Social security must be applied for at least three months before your 65th birthday (or three months before you want to begin receiving social security benefits). Most of the time, you are better off to take the high-income earning spouse's social security benefits at age 70 and the lower-income earning spouse's benefits at age 65 to receive full benefits from both. It may be necessary for the high income earner to "file and suspend" his or her social security benefits. If you began taking your partial social security benefits and have now decided that you want to wait until age 65 to receive any more, you can file a "withdrawal of claim" with the Social Security Administration and the IRS. If you will be receiving any social security benefits from a deceased spouse, you will get these at age 50 — though not the full amount your partner would have received.

When you are on the verge of retirement, begin considering your Medicare options and filing the necessary paperwork to receive it. Do not look at Medicare as a government handout — it can be useful, especially given the rising costs of private health insurance and the decline of employer-sponsored health care for retirees. Medicare is available once you reach age 65 and has three different components: Part A, hospital insurance; Part B, medical insurance; and prescription drug coverage. Part A does not normally require a premium (paid for through payroll taxes during employment). In order to qualify for Part A, you must meet certain conditions — this type of health insurance will mostly cover the costs of inpatient hospital care and hospice care. Part B normally requires a monthly premium and covers doctors' visits, outpatient care, some home care, and some physical therapy. The prescription drug coverage requires a monthly premium and as of

2006, is available to anyone with Medicare. It assists in lowering the cost of prescription drugs.

A Tip from TIAA-CREF

In order to create an "income floor" that you cannot outlive, consider using some of your retirement funds to create a lifetime annuity income. Consider evaluating your risk of outliving your income and assets by using a planning tool that incorporates "probabilities" (Monte Carlo Programming) that examine the impact of variability of returns (bull and bear markets) and the impact of inflation spikes. In other words, one that does not assume you earn a constant rate each year of retirement, which is unrealistic.

Fast Fact

For those looking to retire soon, mortgages are expected to become a major problem — in 2001, according to the Joint Center on Housing Studies at Harvard University, a study found that in 60 percent of homes where the head of household is age 55 to 64, there is an outstanding balance on the mortgage — this climbed nearly 15 percent from 1989 to 2001.

Fast Fact

According to the Employee Benefit Research Institute, two-thirds of those in the job force over age 55 have less than $100,000 put aside for retirement; 56 percent of current retirees have only $50,000 to get them through the rest of retirement — even though this is hard to believe, many people can live comfortably on this by taking on an enjoyable part-time job, moving to a less expensive house or part of the country, or using other measures to make ends meet.

Fast Fact

There are Web sites out there that are trying to help retirees get back into the work force — for both the retirees' benefit and for the company's benefit of stemming the "brain drain.

Fast Fact

The state of California has set up a Web site for their employees called Boomerang, **www.boomerang.ca.gov**, that allows retirees to post a "resume" that indicates what work they had previously done, what they enjoy doing now, and how many hours a week they want to spend working for the state. Government departments are then able to go online and find retirees to fill employment gaps.

Action Item

When you retire, do not withdraw too much early on. Do not decide to spend all your money at once, or you will not have enough to do what you want later in retirement — and you might not be able to pay for important emergency events, like health care or other long-term care.

Chapter 10 Summary

- As you draw closer to your retirement date, you will want to begin making plans about exactly when you will need your retirement funds and when you will begin taking withdrawals.

- Take social security or pensions into account when you make this decision — it is better for you to live off of social security money before taking retirement account withdrawals, if possible, because then your account can continue to grow and accumulate money.

- Remember, the earlier you take your social security benefits before age 65, the less you will receive.

- Do not consider Medicare to be a government handout — you will benefit from it in the long-term.

11 *Saving At Any Age*

In this chapter, you will learn:

- The benefits of saving when you are young

- How to squeeze a little extra money into your retirement account

- What to do if you have not started saving and are nearing retirement age

18 to 24 Years Old

When you are young, you likely do not think much about saving for the future, but this is the best time to begin developing good saving habits that will help you in the future. Small steps will benefit you in the end. When you turn 18, you may begin getting many credit card offers, but choose wisely and spend wisely on your credit cards. Your credit rating will follow you for many years and can affect the interest rate you get on a mortgage or a car. Look at your options when it comes to renting, buying, or living at home for a few more years. If you are living with someone else, you have a chance to build a larger savings fund that you can use as a down payment or as extra money for a 401(k) plan if your future employer offers one. The most important thing you can do at this time is save and budget — develop good habits now, and you are on your way to being rich in retirement.

A Tip from Vanguard

Attention young investors: Vanguard would recommend that all investors separate aspects of investing into "controllable" and "uncontrollable." The biggest factor out of their control is the market's return. Investors are likely to be disappointed if they set a return target for their equity portfolios for a given year because the long-run average return from U.S. stocks (approximately 10 percent since 1926) has not been delivered in a smooth, reliable fashion. Stocks — even well-diversified stock funds — are risky, and the year-to-year returns for the market are unpredictable.

25 Years Old

At age 25, you may be thinking more about moving up the career ladder, getting married, paying off college loans, or buying your first home than you are about your retirement. But this is the time to start seriously considering it and investing. Do not miss out. As mentioned earlier, growing your 401(k) nest egg is not always about how much you invest in your account, but how long you invest for. At age 25, you still have approximately 40 years of investing ahead of you.

At this point in your life, it is vital that you sit down and look at your saving and spending habits. Make a list of necessary items and nice-to-have items. Once you have looked all of this information over, make a long-term savings plan. This is not the only time in your life that you will be intensely going over this information — it is necessary to look at your habits and your plan and update it to reflect any changes in inflation and your job, for example.

If you want to have a million dollars in your retirement account by age 65, you will need to save $286 per month, which includes adjustments for inflation. This is the time when you want to go for high-risk investments, such as domestic and international stocks. You will have some time to recover with safer options in the event the market takes a serious downturn, but bear in mind that it runs in cycles, so do not bail out too early. If you can invest more than this amount, by all means do so. At least make sure you are investing enough in your retirement account to get the maximum amount of employer-matching contributions available to you.

There are other ways that you can begin contributing more to your account at this time if you just focus on saving money. If you already have a mortgage and this is what takes away from your retirement savings, consider refinancing — as long as interest rates are below your current rate. This will help you consolidate your debts and lower what you pay each month, meaning more money to invest. You can also consider debt consolidation or re-budget until you are down to spending money only on the necessities. But be smart about all this — do not cut back on all your payments just to have a little extra in retirement savings. It is important to pay down your high-interest or excessive credit card debt before investing more money in your 401(k) plan.

When you are ten years or more away from retirement, you can plan to be invested entirely in stock mutual funds because, although your portfolio will be volatile, it will, in the long run, outperform other forms of investments. Plus, if you want the best rate of return, you need to take a risk.

A Tip from ShareBuilder

Start saving in your company's 401(k) or in an individual IRA account the moment you start your first job — be it a small amount or more. The habit of starting and making it automatic is a key to many people's financial success. The advantage of having money working for you for the next 40-plus years is something that is tough to try and beat if you wait even five to ten years.

CASE STUDY: DONALD BENNYHOFF, SENIOR INVESTMENT ANALYST

Vanguard P.O. Box 1110
Valley Forge, PA 19482
www.vanguard.com
Linda_S_Wolohan@Vanguard.com
1-800-523-1036 – Voice
1-610-669-6840 – Fax
Donald Bennyhoff
Senior Investment Analyst

Investors tend to be overconfident in their investing skills and underestimate how difficult it is to outperform the market. The market return is not just a number; it is a reflection of the collective performance of investors, nonprofessionals and professionals alike, across the globe. Since such a large portion of investment assets are under the influence of professionals, with ample resources, education, and experience, investors should ask themselves a tough question: What gives me a reliable advantage over the rest of the people trying to outperform? Since the probability and consequences of underperforming the market tend to be more significant than those for outperforming the market, we recommend that investors invest in funds that track broad market indexes and take a long-term approach. A

CASE STUDY: DONALD BENNYHOFF, SENIOR INVESTMENT ANALYST

simple, disciplined investment strategy provides the highest probability for success.

The good news is that most of the factors that matter are well within investors' control. Start with a well-thought-out investment strategy that considers your individual objectives and risk tolerance. Use asset allocation and diversification to help manage the risks that are inherent with investing. Choose cost-effective funds that keep expense ratios low. In taxable accounts, choose funds that will keep capital gain distributions to a minimum. And rebalance periodically to maintain the asset allocation and risk posture that you decided was appropriate. Invest diligently and systematically, if possible, through employer-sponsored retirement plans, and invest as much as you can. A comfortable retirement depends on the investor's contributions — the market cannot be relied upon to overcome a lifetime of undersaving.

You never know when the current Wall Street darling will fall out of favor, turning your outsized gains into outsized losses. For example, investors who poured money into technology-focused funds in the late 1990s can testify to the dangers of tilting a portfolio heavily toward one type of investment. Many people had too little invested in the relative underperformers of the time, particularly value, small-cap, international, and REIT stocks — the very areas that outperformed later. A key lesson is that no one type of investment should have too much — or too little — weight in a portfolio.

Asset allocation is the cornerstone of good investment practice. The ratio of investment assets that make up a portfolio can vary significantly, even among investors who might be the same age. Other factors beside age — such as risk tolerance, investment horizon, tax sensitivity, desired or required return goals, and investment experience — can all affect how the investor's portfolio should be constructed. Generally speaking, it is not uncommon for younger investors to have equity-centric asset allocations to promote growth of the portfolio and contend with the erosion of purchasing power due to inflation. Alternatively,

CASE STUDY: DONALD BENNYHOFF, SENIOR INVESTMENT ANALYST

older investors, particularly those in retirement, may prefer lower-equity allocations to moderate the volatility of their portfolios.

Vanguard has a list of asset allocation guidelines by age bands, but it is important to note that age is only one factor that should be considered in the asset allocation decision. Other important factors include goals, the time horizon for when you need the money, and your risk tolerance. So while these recommendations may be appropriate for some investors, they will not be for all.

Once you have established a diversified portfolio, you will want to make sure you do not lose the balance you have worked to create. That will mean periodic rebalancing — shifting money from one type of investment to another — to ensure that you continue to hold the mix of stock, bond, and short-term investments that you deemed appropriate for yourself.

Unless you are in a life cycle fund, you will need to monitor your portfolio periodically to make sure it has not strayed considerably from your target allocation among stocks, bonds, and cash investments. Just as your car can get out of alignment, so can your investment portfolio — due simply to the movements of the stock and bond markets. Check your asset-class weightings periodically and rebalance whenever any asset class has strayed meaningfully from its target allocation: Our research has shown that a deviation of more than five percentage points is a reasonable rule-of-thumb. Better yet, use cash flows either into or out of the portfolio as a rebalancing opportunity to minimize the need for larger, potentially more tax-inefficient reallocations.

35 Years Old

At this point, according to Kiplinger's, you will need $671 per month to go into your retirement account. This might seem like a hefty sum, especially if you are raising a family, helping elderly parents, and trying to set aside money for your children's college funds. This brings up a good question — are you better off helping your children pay for college or having extra money to put into your retirement account? While the answer may sound cruel, saving for retirement is certainly the better option; you can finance an education, but no one is going to give you grants and loans for retirement.

If you are still coming up short after looking over your spending and saving habits, consider asking for a raise or a promotion at work. If one is not available, and does not look like it is in your future, consider changing jobs if there is a better, more lucrative option available for you, especially if the new job offers a better 401(k) or other retirement savings plan.

45 Years Old

If you have saved nothing up to this point, you will need to save $1,698 per month. But do not worry — there are ways to save and cut corners, even at 45. If you spent time getting a masters degree or a Ph.D., or even if you have performed specialized research or know a good deal about a certain topic, consider opening your own business on the side. If you have an expertise, become a consultant. If you are an expert seamstress, open a weekend business. If you like to write, consider freelancing.

If you have children who will be going to college or getting jobs soon, think about encouraging them to move out (only if they seem to be overstaying their welcome) or charge them for rent and utilities. Not only are freeloading young adults bad for your retirement savings and finances, they are not learning about financial responsibility they will need to save for retirement.

Once you reach age 50, you can begin playing catch up by contributing an extra $5,000 per year to your 401(k) account. Also, if you already have a retirement account, this is a good time to consider rebalancing it to ensure you are gradually moving toward more conservative investment options.

50 Years Old

When you turn 50, the government lets you play catch-up with your retirement funds, whether you have been making the maximum allowed contribution each year or not. Congress set up this provision because they assume that many people have not been contributing enough to their 401(k) plans at a younger age, whether because they just were not playing smart with their money or had to leave the workforce for a while and were unable to contribute to any account at that time. The law allowing for the catch-up contribution was adopted in 2002, and some employers have been slow to adopt it, so be sure your employer provides for the new provision in your plan. After you hit 50, you can contribute, as of 2008, an extra $5,500 per year to your 401(k) account. Raising the contribution limit to $5,500 does not mean your employer now has to contribute less. Only your personal pre-tax contributions are counted toward this limit, as long as you hold a 401(k) or 403(b) plan. If you happen to hold a 457 plan, your contributions will be added to your employer's contributions and, as of 2009, cannot be more than $25,500 (the normal contribution limit plus the $5,500 catch-up).

A Tip from ShareBuilder

Take advantage of catch-up amounts the government allows to help you reach your goals if you think you have fallen behind. Once you are 50, you can contribute an extra $5,500 per year to your 401(k) (the limit increased to $20,500 a year for 2008 and will increase again to $22,000 in 2009) or in an IRA where can put in an extra $1,000 a year (up to $6,000 a year for 2008).

55 Years Old

If, up to this point, you have not invested a dime in your retirement, you will need to save $5,466 per month. Even if you cannot set aside this large sum each month, it is time to stop making excuses and start investing. There is still plenty of time for you to invest, and you are better off having some money in retirement than no money at all. If you are willing to work at it and cut corners, you can retire rich.

The first thing you should do is plan not to spend any extra money — put it all into your 401(k) or other retirement plan, and try to contribute the maximum allowed amount. If you happen to be one of the lucky few who can contribute more than the maximum, contribute to multiple accounts, but always invest first in the one that offers added monetary benefits, such as employer-matching contributions. This is also a good time to review the federal government's 401(k) catch-up rules.

If you still are not finding enough money to contribute to your plan, consider changing employers or taking on a second job if you can get a better retirement account. Consider working past age 65 (you may want something to cure you from boredom in retirement) or even moving into a smaller home, if you are still paying your mortgage.

A Tip from Vanguard

Attention older investors: This is addressed to investors about to enter retirement. Do not blindly overweight your portfolio with bonds — in other words, do not trade the income you had from your salary with the income you expect to get from bonds. This can lead to a less diversified portfolio than many investors should have and may jeopardize the portfolio's ability to outpace inflation. This is important because life expectancy tables suggest that for a 65-year-old couple, there is a 72 percent chance that at least one will live to age 85, and an almost 20 percent chance that one will live to age 95. Today, you should plan conservatively, and plan on your retirement income lasting 25 or 30 years. For most investors, a meaningful, well-diversified allocation to equities is prudent.

65 Years and Older

Believe it or not, there are still choices you need to make when you reach retirement age. This is a good time to again consider whether you can afford to retire, or if you need to continue working or take on a part-time job. Think about when the best time to take your social security benefits is and apply for Medicare to help you save some money on medical costs.

If you still have money in your 401(k) account, and intend to leave it for awhile, rebalance the funds into low-risk investments. Also, begin thinking about when you will make withdrawals and how much you will be taking each time.

Action Item

When you do decide to retire, there are a few questions you should ask yourself to decide whether you are truly ready.

1. Do I have cash reserves that I can use to delay making withdrawals from my 401(k) for as long as possible and enough to wait and take my social security payments until I receive full benefits?

2. Have I considered increased medical costs and planned accordingly?

3. Have I planned for withdrawals, and will each last me long enough to support the type of retirement I plan to have?

4. Will I be able to make it for many years in retirement without having to go back to the job force?

5. Have I made a realistic budget plan for the future?

6. Are there added expenses in the near future that I can foresee, and have I planned for them?

7. Have I made a plan for unforeseen expenses?

Once you have retired, do not be surprised if you feel out of place, especially if you still have many friends and family members in the job force. Many retirees end up entering the job market again, whether on a full- or part-time basis with their previous employer or a new one, and some even set up their own businesses — and many are finding that they are being welcomed back with open arms. The American Association of Retired People (AARP) has found that 69 percent of baby boomers plan to stay in the job market past retirement age. Employers have begun seeing this as a boom to their business, fearful of a brain drain that may have taken place when all the baby boomers retired. A record 24.6 million of those over age 55 were in the workforce as of 2006. To encourage employees to work past retirement, employers are offering more flexible working hours, shorter schedules, or jobs that can travel with them if they have summer and winter homes after retirement. Other employers see retirees as a mixed blessing — they can be a drain on benefits and also require higher salaries than their younger counterparts, but their work ethic often matches or exceeds that of younger workers.

Retirees, on the other hand, benefit from returning to work by being able to continue to contribute to a 401(k) or other retirement account, and also have extra money on the side to pay for vacations and other extras without having to dip into cash savings or retirement funds. Even just a couple extra years in the workforce can significantly affect the amount you have in your 401(k) when you decide to leave the workforce permanently. Plus, as the earlier table indicates, if you can hold off on drawing Social Security, you will be able to receive the full amount rather than a reduced early check.

Retirees who want to continue working, but would rather be their own boss, are also finding a niche for themselves. A business called Bizstarters (**www.bizstarters.com**) helps those 50 and older launch and grow businesses, many of which are Web-based. Half of all small business owners are over age 50. In addition, if you open your own business without any employees, you can create a solo 401(k) account where you can contribute about $50,000 per year.

When you do finally decide to retire for good, use your cash reserves for living expenses before dipping into your 401(k) or other retirement account. Your 401(k) can still earn interest, and you do not want to lose out on gaining every last penny you can for later in life. If you find out you do not have enough cash reserves on hand and need to begin digging into your retirement account early, you may need to withdraw conservatively or consider changing your lifestyle down the road — buying a smaller house, taking a later retirement, or spending less.

The most important thing, though, is that you know what you want to do when you retire. It will do you no good to begin making last-minute decisions about withdrawals or more stable investments — this should be something that goes into your long-term plan and something you reconsider as you draw nearer to retirement. Be sure you have an emergency fund for any unexpected expenses, and check in on your other accounts to see how much money you have coming to you, how it will be paid, and how you can make withdrawals, just to name a few things — this should include a good look at your social security account.

Considering Social Security

Even though it is not recommended that you rely on social security to cover your basic needs in retirement, it is important to know at least a little bit about it. As of 2006, 6.2 percent will be taken from your wages every year, and your employer will give another 6.2 percent to the Social Security Administration. This money is being "saved" for your retirement. Some of this money goes toward paying for the social security benefits of those who are currently retired, while the other part of the money goes to a social security trust fund that, in theory, is supposed to be building up a stock for you and others who will retire at some point. Unfortunately, this money is not enough to cover retirement for everyone, but there is no telling when the money will run out. It may not be available when you retire, even though you paid into it. It is possible that in the future, either taxes will go up or benefits will be reduced.

When you retire, and if you are lucky enough to receive social security by the time you do, it is important for you to not forget that the benefits you will receive are dependent on how much you earned when you were in the job force. The more you make while you are employed, the more you will receive in social security benefits. Once you pass a certain age, the government will begin sending you statements regarding how much money you will receive at age 62, if you choose to take an early retirement, and how much you will receive at full retirement age (65 to 67, depending on when you were born — see the previous chart). You cannot begin taking social security payments until age 62, and, normally, you must begin taking them before you reach age 70. The longer you wait to take your social security payments (up until you turn 70), the more you will receive at each payment. A social security warning: You will lose $1 of social security money for every $2 earned if you work and take social security between ages 62 and 66.

You would be wise to wait as long as possible to take your social security benefits and also to consider social security funds extra money rather than the money you will need to pay your bills in retirement. Many who are entering the job force now do not know whether they will have social security dollars available to them, so it would be hard for them to think that the government will be taking care of them through social security — this generation will likely be completely dependent on their own 401(k) or other retirement savings accounts.

If you die, your husband or wife will have to decide whether he or she wants to take 100 percent of the benefits you were receiving before your death, or 100 percent of the benefits he or she is receiving. Your spouse cannot receive both sets of benefits.

Retirement Myth

Social security is going to run out, and I will be left without any of the money that came from my paycheck for so long.

Even if the amount being doled out to workers decreases, there will still likely be something left in the social security pot. Congress has been involved in a significant amount of decision making lately regarding this problem, and one thing they might decide to do is cut the benefit for higher-income earners in order to assist those who need it more. But you should not be counting on social security in the first place — you should be putting enough away for retirement so that you can live comfortably without it.

Common Saving Tips

There are some common cutbacks everyone can make in different areas. During the especially tough economic times right now, it is good to have a sound savings strategy.

Action Item
Always have an emergency fund.

Fast Fact
A 2008 Transamerica Center for Retirement Studies report found that the number of working Americans who said that "paying off debt" was their greatest financial concern climbed from just under one-fifth to just under one-third since the 2007 survey.

Fast Fact
According to Transamerica, more people say that they would choose a higher-paying job over one that offers better retirement benefits.

Food

Saving on food is easier than you think. By making fewer grocery trips, you can cut down on the amount that you spend — people commonly buy more than they intend to when they go to the grocery store, so frequent small trips can lead to spending more. Eating out can also be a big drain on your income. If you bring a brown bag lunch to work and eat dinner out less frequently, you will save quite a bit during the year. Clipping the Sunday coupons is an excellent way to save — even though it may seem like just pennies to you at the time.

Transportation

If you currently have a gas-guzzling large car or truck, consider downsizing to something more fuel-efficient and buying something used to save on the monthly payments. When you get your car insurance, consider eliminating the collision insurance because it can, in the end, cost you more in insurance than your car is worth. If you are a person who likes to use the highest octane gas for the best performance, consider switching to the cheapest gas you can buy. Also, shop around for your gas; do not just buy it at the station closest to your house because it is the most convenient. Every penny you can save is another penny that you can put into your retirement account.

Travel and Entertainment

For most people, travel and entertainment is something that can be completely cut from a normal budget, but if you insist on keeping these categories, consider traveling in the off-season, when you can get some of the best rates. Buy package deals through airlines, hotels, or travel brokers so that you can bundle the trip and save. Consider staying local for your weekend getaway — explore some place you have never been before that is just around the corner. Plus, if nothing else, think about staying in a hostel or camping ground before you go straight to that four-star hotel. Many large cities offer group accommodations for a fraction of the cost of a hotel.

As for entertainment, consider renting movies from your library rather than at the video store and borrowing books rather than buying a new one each month. If you have a stadium or other large entertainment venue near you, consider volunteering or working there to earn free tickets or other incentives. Take advantage of any entertainment discount you can get, even if it means going to the movies in the afternoon rather than the evening. If you can get a large group together to go to a theatre show or to the movies — many places offer group rates that will take a certain percentage off each ticket price. Finally, drop your gym membership. You can get workout DVDs and minimal gym equipment for a fraction of the price you pay each year to go to the gym, and you get the added bonus of being able to work out in your own home.

Other Savings

If it is available in your area, bundle your phone, Internet, and cable together rather than purchasing each separately. In many cases, this can save a significant amount of money. In any financial matters, be sure to keep a low balance on your credit cards, and always call your credit card or loan provider to see if they can offer you a lower interest rate. Consider transferring the balance of one debt onto another credit card — this way, you can consolidate your payments and get the benefit of a lower rate because you always want to transfer your higher interest rates onto a lower interest rate card. Finally, use free automated teller machines (ATMs) whenever possible. While the $2–$3 service fee may not seem like much at the time, it can add up.

Fast Fact

According to a poll by AARP, a third of retirees say their debt levels are a problem, while 7 percent consider them to be a major problem.

Fast Fact

According to the Employee Benefit Research Institute, between 1992 and 2001, the number of people age 65 and over who were filing for bankruptcy jumped 213 percent. One reason for the spike — health care costs. During the same timeframe, households headed by someone over age 75 rose 160 percent, to just over $20,000.

Older Investor Myths

There are many myths or excuses that older investors tend to believe and use as reasons not to begin a retirement savings plan.

One myth many older investors believe is that because they did not start saving sooner, they might as well not start when they are near retirement. It is never too late to begin a savings plan — every little bit helps. Of course, the earlier you save, and the more often you save, the more you are going to have when you eventually retire. But just being older does not mean you cannot make compounding interest work for you. If you can, begin making the maximum allowed contributions to your 401(k) plan or any other retirement account available to you. If you have money left over, open a second retirement account, such as an IRA or Roth IRA. Be sure you are taking advantage of any extra contributions you can make, as well as the contributions your employer makes. Do not fall into the trap and believe that because you did not start a savings plan earlier, you should invest aggressively now. Because you are closer to retirement, you will have less chance to make up for major losses in the market and can end up right back where you started. Instead of trying to compensate with investments, save more and consider working to a later age. Or, cut back on what you believe you will be able to do in retirement.

Another myth that deals with aging is the belief that you will not need your retirement savings for very long. Many people are living well into their 80s and 90s today, thanks to advances in science and medicine. Make sure that you will have a steady income stream for all of your retirement, not just the first ten years.

Odd as it sounds, diversification leads into another myth — that you must spread your money into many different funds to be properly diversified. It is true that you want to spread your money around well in order to ensure its safety in the market, but when you are late to investing, and do not have much in an account, you will be spreading yourself too thin to make any sort of return on your investments. Instead, you are better off with a target-date fund or a mutual fund, which will buy many investments for you but pool your money with many other investors to ensure a larger return.

Finally, those who have been investing for a long time and those who are new to investing believe that because stocks hold a higher risk, they should immediately sell off any stocks they have upon retirement. This is not a safe option, especially because it can cause you to outlive the money you have saved. Remember that even though you are retired, inflation will still continue, and if you are heavily invested in safe options, you may not be able to outpace, or even keep pace, with it. This is not to say that you should be heavily invested in stocks, but your account should remain well diversified.

Fast Fact

According to Transamerica, many more people are reporting that they do not save for retirement because they need to pay off debt.

Chapter 11 Summary

- There are multiple ways that you can cut back on your spending to ensure that you have more money to put aside into your 401(k) or other retirement account. You can save on your telephone or Internet, dining out, entertainment, travel, and especially food.

- Social security will be available to you when you retire, but it should not be your only source of income in retirement. There is no guarantee on whether that account will be around in the future.

- When you are young, begin making plans for how you will save throughout your job, and begin lowering credit card debt.

- The younger you are, the better off you are starting to build your nest egg, because you will have 40 or more years left in the workforce before you need to make retirement withdrawals — plenty of time to save enough to retire rich.

- When you are young, it is also a good time to get in the habit of saving and lowering your spending.

- When you reach age 50, the government allows you to play catch-up with your retirement account, even if you have been contributing the maximum thus far, by allowing you to contribute an extra $5,500 each year to your 401(k).

- No matter how old you are, you need to save — if you think you are too old or young to begin saving for retirement, stop making excuses; you cannot retire rich if you do not save.

- When you do draw close to retirement, think about whether you can retire or whether you need to remain in the job force.

- Those who are older when they begin saving believe there are many reasons why they should not even bother opening a retirement account — none of them are good reasons.

12

Other Retirement Account Options

In this chapter, you will learn:

- How to deal with a below-par retirement account

- When IRAs might be useful

- What to do if you are self-employed and want to open a retirement account

Making the Best of a Bad Situation

If you decide that the plan you are offered by your employer is not that good, do not stop contributing, and if you have not already done so, begin contributing to another account. Chances are, you like your job enough that you are not going to leave and begin hunting for a new job just because of the 401(k) plan, although you may want to hire a professional financial planner who can best help you decide what you need to do with this bad account to reach your retirement goals. Also, do not simply decide to gamble with the bad plan and put a little bit of your account dollars into each investment. This is not a good way to earn any money, and it does not provide you much stability during a market downturn.

Some jobs have restricted 401(k) plans that offer few investment options and are often especially conservative. You may be faced with options such as conservative stocks, bonds, or money market funds. As mentioned earlier, you can try to get a group of employees together and lobby your employer for a better plan, but it is more likely that you will need to deal with what you are offered. If you find yourself in this type of situation, be sure to choose the investments that most closely reflect the plan that you have made for retirement. If you were planning to invest in high-risk stocks, find the most high-risk stocks you can, even though you are investing in a conservative plan. If you need to, look outside your own 401(k) account for additional investment options. Also, if it is bad enough, you will most likely want to consider making investments completely separate of your employer-sponsored 401(k). If you have to go this route, make sure your investments are not the same as what you are being offered in your plan — try to diversify and look for something higher-risk, such as municipal bonds or international stock. Or you can consider opening your own IRA or other retirement account.

IRAs

An IRA is good for people who are self-employed or are not eligible for a 401(k) retirement plan or who just need an extra place for additional retirement savings after maxing out 401(k) contributions. In this type of account, money grows tax-deferred — much like in a 401(k) account — which is why it is known as a tax-sheltered retirement plan.

There are multiple types of IRAs, including the Roth IRA, which is tax-free, and the education IRA, which can help you save money for secondary education expenses for you or your dependents. IRAs are set up through mutual fund companies, banks, or stockbrokers.

There are stipulations for being able to contribute. You must have earned income in the year you plan to invest, meaning you cannot just be living off interest and investing that. You must be under 70 and a half years old; you cannot open a new IRA account after this age. Unlike a 401(k) account, in which you can make extra contributions when you reach a certain age, the IRA does not allow for any catch-up contributions, no matter how old you are or how little you have contributed in the past. Any contributions you make to your IRA account will grow tax-free until you begin making withdrawals. In some cases, you will be able to deduct your IRA contributions from your taxes for an added benefit. Do note, though, that there is no borrowing from an IRA allowed, and any early withdrawals will be subject to the same 10 percent penalty and taxes that are applicable to a 401(k) account.

For those who are self-employed, there is a special type of IRA known as the Simplified Employee Pension plan that you can choose to sign up for among other options — see the end of this chapter for more information.

An IRA is considered a trust account. This means that the bank or other financial institution that holds your IRA must be approved by the FDIC and maintain your account. Any necessary paperwork for your account will be taken care of by your account trustee or custodian and will be filed with the Department of Labor and the IRS. The custodian or trustee will be the person who invests your money in any funds you have chosen and will ensure that when you choose to make a withdrawal, that money gets to you. He or she will not force you to contribute to your account — or make sure that you do so — so that responsibility will still rest with you.

Your IRA can be invested in many different places unless you hold an education IRA, which limits your investment options. Some employees are able to open an IRA through their employer, which will allow them to make automatic contributions from their paycheck each pay period. Nonetheless, with a company-sponsored IRA, your investment choices will be limited. If you have an IRA through a bank, you may be able to set up an automatic contribution from your bank account or paycheck. This account will normally be invested in a money market fund or CD because the money cannot be easily moved around and is relatively stable.

If you are unsure about investing in an IRA, the bank IRA is most likely a good choice for you because it is normally a low-risk, short-term investment. Therefore, if you decide you do not like the account, you can leave it after a year or so without paying an early withdrawal penalty, or you can simply roll it over into another CD, if you are happy with this investment option.

A mutual fund IRA is offered by most mutual fund companies, and you will have a multitude of investment options, though they will all be within the mutual fund. As the market and your stages of life change, you are able to move your money into and out of a money market

IRA without having to pay penalties or income taxes. The mutual fund IRA is a recommended choice for new investors because it is easy to choose a few investments and have a well-diversified portfolio. Finally, a self-directed IRA is for those who are well-versed in investing and do not want many constraints on their investment choices. Through this type of mutual fund, you can choose to invest in a mutual fund or in individual stocks, bonds, securities, or CDs. There are a lot of fees involved in a self-directed IRA, and you may have to pay a setup fee.

It is important to know who controls your IRA account and takes your contributions. You want to know who this person is, because you need to know who to turn to when you want to reallocate your investments or just check in to ensure that everything is being invested the way you had hoped. The custodian of your account will ensure that any money you put into the account is invested in the way you stipulate and will also ensure that when you want to take money out of the account, you receive the proper distribution amounts at the right time. No one, though, will make sure that you are investing in your account. Unlike a 401(k) account, your money will not be automatically taken from your paycheck and put into an IRA, so you need to make the decision and take the initiative to put the money in yourself.

If you decide that you want to convert your 401(k) into an IRA — because you are changing jobs or are leaving the job force — you must do so within 60 days of receiving your 401(k) funds (if the money is coming to you in check form and not going straight to your new IRA). There is a limit on what you can and cannot roll over from a 401(k) to an IRA. You cannot roll over any after-tax contributions, but you can roll over pre-tax contributions and any interest earnings on all contributions to the account. To set up a rollover from a 401(k) to an IRA, you must either allow your employer to directly roll over the investment without the money ever touching your hands, or you can get a check from your employer that is made out to the financial institution that will hold your IRA account. As previously mentioned, if you let your employer make the check out to you rather than to the financial institution the money is going to, 20 percent will be taken out for taxes, and you will be responsible to pay that money back.

Investing your IRA account is as important as investing your 401(k) or other retirement account. It is imperative, just like in 401(k) investment, that you do not forget to diversify your investments to properly balance your risk and ensure the best rate of return. One of the benefits of an IRA is that you can move your money from investment to investment with relative ease should you decide that you are not happy with your current investment allocation. It will be the easiest for you if you choose to move your money into another fund held within the organization that holds your IRA. If you decide that you want to invest outside of this organization, you will have to do a little paperwork. All transfers occur tax-free by order of the federal government, and you must either do an asset transfer or a rollover. An asset transfer occurs when you move your IRA account dollars from one financial group to another, while a rollover occurs when a check is made out directly to you, and you take that check and create another IRA or put the check into an existing IRA. If you choose to do an asset transfer, you will take your entire IRA account and give it to a new custodian or investment company. You will not have to pay an early withdrawal penalty or any income taxes on what you transfer. Normally, you will not have to worry about transferring the funds yourself, as your new and old custodians will work together to move your funds. A rollover happens when you take the funds out of your IRA directly before putting it into another IRA rather than doing an asset transfer. If you choose to do this, your old IRA account funds must go into the new account within 60 days or you will owe early withdrawal penalties and any necessary income taxes.

Unlike other retirement accounts, an IRA does not allow you to take out a loan against yourself. However, every 12 months, you can withdraw money from the account — even if you are younger than age 59 and a half — as long as you put the money back in the account within 60 days. If you do, you will not be charged any taxes or penalties. If you do not, the government will levy a hefty penalty, and you will be responsible for paying any income tax due on the amount you withdrew.

Before now, 457 plans could not be rolled over into an IRA, and 403(b) retirement accounts could only be rolled over to an IRA. In addition, any after-tax contributions were required to be withdrawn before a rollover of pre-tax contributions could take place. Now, all these accounts, and any pre-tax or after-tax contributions, can be rolled over. However, Roth IRAs cannot be turned back into traditional IRAs or Roth 401(k)s. Only funds that can be taxed are able to be rolled over to an IRA. Pre-tax money can also be left in the retirement account offered by your employer — an option you may choose because it will allow you to bypass the pro rate rule. If you choose to convert your retirement account into an IRA, you will benefit from the lack of rules and regulations. A rollover is known as an eligible rollover distribution (ERD). Any required minimum distributions cannot be rolled over from your current retirement account to an IRA; you must withdraw those funds as indicated in your 401(k) or other retirement account plan rules.

When you choose to retire or leave your current employer, you might choose to roll the money over into an IRA because your beneficiaries could keep any money in the account after your death, where it would continue to grow. Your beneficiaries must still take the required minimum distributions. An IRA can fold into your entire estate well after your death. Other benefits of an IRA include: more investment choices; the ability to put some of your IRA money into an annuity; no restrictions on withdrawals; the ability to consolidate any retirement plans you hold; and ease of moving from an IRA to another plan. If you choose to stay in your former employer's plan once you have retired or left the company, you have the benefit of being able to borrow money from yourself, and if you continue to work past the normal retirement date, you can hold off until age 70 and a half to take your required minimum distribution.

When planning how you will pay your estate taxes and handle your estate upon your death, you may want to consider splitting your IRA into multiple accounts with beneficiaries for each. This also means that you will pay lower taxes. But be careful choosing beneficiaries from the person and non-person groups and mixing those; this can become confusing for you and your beneficiaries. Instead, split the IRA and have your spouse be the sole beneficiary of one (or whomever you want to name) and your children's trust fund as another.

A Tip from ShareBuilder

IRAs can play a great role in helping Americans save on a tax-deferred basis for retirement. Like a 401(k) account, earnings grow tax-deferred until you make withdrawals upon reaching 59 and a half. It is important to mention Roth options, both in IRAs and 401(k)s. These work in the reverse of traditional IRAs and 401(k)s. You pay taxes before contributing, but then you will not be taxed again on the monies, earnings and all. For those who expect to be in a higher tax bracket, or expect tax rates to rise, it can be a smart way to save.

Non-deductible IRA

Another type of IRA that may be available to you is known as the non-deductible IRA. This is a good place to invest your money if, for some reason, you are not able to make tax-deductible contributions to a traditional IRA. Any money you put into the account will be tax-deferred until you decide to begin taking withdrawals. Non-deductible IRAs incur a significant amount of paperwork for the IRS, especially if you hold the non-deductible IRA in addition to a traditional IRA. The nice part about this type of account is that as long as you keep all of your paperwork, any of your original contributions that are in the account will not be taxed because they already have been, and you cannot be double taxed unless you do not give your IRA provider the proper paperwork. If you hold a traditional IRA or non-deductible IRA you will need to add both accounts together to figure out what you owe in taxes and how much of your money should be withdrawn during each payment you take from the account. These accounts will not be joined physically at this time, just on paper for ease of calculation.

Roth IRA

The Roth IRA, named for Senator William Roth, was introduced in 1998 as an alternative to a traditional IRA to ensure that more people are eligible to put away retirement savings. This is because the income limitations on contributions are higher in Roth IRA accounts than in other retirement accounts. As long as you meet certain income requirements, you can contribute to a Roth IRA account, even if you are already contributing to an employer-sponsored plan. A Roth IRA is different from most retirement accounts because you will pay the income tax up-front on the account in order for it to remain income-tax-free forever (even when you begin taking withdrawals), meaning you can earn more over time.

There are two different types of Roth IRAs: Roth IRA contributions and Roth IRA conversions. In a Roth IRA account, you are able to contribute $5,000 per year if your income is below $99,000 if you are single, or if your income is under $156,000, if you are married and file your taxes jointly. When you turn 50, your contribution limit is increased $1,000, so you would be able to contribute $6,000 per year. Anyone, no matter what age, can contribute to a Roth contribution IRA. A Roth IRA conversion gives you the ability to make considerable amount of money, but you must be able to pay the taxes on it first. You can convert as much money as you want from another retirement account into a Roth IRA conversion, and as of May 17, 2006, everyone can make a conversion, beginning in 2010, when income restrictions are dropped. But if you want to make a conversion now, you will need to lower your income to under $100,000 per year. One way to do this is by contributing more to another tax-deferred plan, but do not try to reduce your income to means you cannot get by on.

In order to convert money to a Roth IRA, you have to get the money out of your other retirement account and transfer it or have the money transferred for you, just like with other retirement account conversions. But the Roth IRA offers another option — if you already have an IRA with the company you want to open a Roth IRA with, you can simply call the company and ask for the account to be retitled to a Roth. Of course, you will have to pay the necessary income taxes. You will only be taxed on the money you decide to convert to a Roth IRA. Be careful when doing this, and do not use money from the retirement account you are rolling over to pay the tax on the Roth IRA. If you do, you might be penalized. If you cannot pay the taxes, do not miss out on the opportunity a Roth IRA presents. Just convert less into a Roth IRA and move more into the account as you are financially able to.

Any contribution made to a Roth IRA is not tax-deductible, but withdrawals are tax-free, as long as the money has been in the account for at least five years and you meet one of the following criteria:

- You are older than 59 and a half

- You have recently been disabled

- You are using the amount you withdraw to purchase your first home

- The money is being paid to a beneficiary after you die

There is no restriction on withdrawals. You do not have to take your money out or stop contributing at any age (unlike with 401(k)s and traditional IRAs). In a traditional IRA, you must begin taking withdrawals at age 70 and a half. Should you decide to roll your traditional IRA into a Roth IRA after this age, you must take that year's required minimum distribution first. If you make an early withdrawal (before age 59 and a half), you will be subject to a 10 percent early withdrawal penalty, unless that money is going toward medical expenses that are more than 7.5 percent of your adjusted gross income, you are unemployed and need to cover medical insurance premiums, or you need to pay higher education expenses for yourself or your dependents. When you do begin withdrawing funds, you will not be taxed until you have withdrawn all your personal contributions and begin to withdraw your earnings on your contributions.

To roll your 401(k) account funds into a Roth IRA or open your own Roth IRA, you must first open a traditional IRA account. If your adjusted gross income is $100,000 or less in the year you decide to make the transition from traditional IRA to Roth IRA, then the transaction will be approved. But when you turn your account into a Roth IRA, you will have to pay the income tax on the traditional IRA at that time; you can lower the amount due all at once by only converting a certain portion from the traditional Roth IRA each year.

Protection on a Roth IRA varies from state to state, so be sure to check on the laws of the state in which you reside. Some states do not protect Roth IRA accounts the way they protect traditional IRA accounts.

Fast Fact

In a traditional IRA, you must choose your beneficiaries by age 70 and a half, at which point they are locked in. This is not the case in a Roth IRA. You can change beneficiaries at any age.

When should you move to an IRA? Commonly, you can assume that 401(k)s are better retirement savings plans than IRAs because the contribution maximum is higher in a 401(k), and you also will be able to receive any employer-matching contributions your company plans to make.

A Tip From Michael J. Fitzgerald

One way to look at using an IRA: "Instead of trying to balance your portfolio in the 401(k) plan, which usually only has 12-15 choices, pick the best of the funds and balance the portfolio with external funds. It does not make sense to put money in underperforming funds."

When you are trying to decide whether to open a Roth IRA, there are a few things that you need to consider, especially if you are choosing between a Roth IRA and a regular 401(k) plan. If you will not be paying the same tax rate when you make contributions to your account as you do when you begin making withdrawals — for example, if you have a change in income between the time you are working and contributing to the account and when you retire and begin taking withdrawals — the Roth IRA is often the better choice. If your tax bracket drops significantly, and you will, therefore, be deducting less in taxes, you will have more money in a 401(k) than you would in a Roth IRA. But, if you went into a higher tax bracket, then you would have to pay more in taxes with a 401(k) account but would have more money in a Roth IRA.

What this means is that, in most cases, the Roth 401(k) is the best bet if you are going to be in the same or a higher tax bracket when you decide to retire, while a regular 401(k) is a good bet for you if you plan to be in a lower tax bracket. Unfortunately, there is not a good way of figuring out what your tax bracket will be once you retire, because many things will affect you at that point, from how much money you will be receiving from 401(k)s, pensions, and other retirement savings accounts to what other taxable income you will have once you retire.

According to an article written by Walter Updegrave, a senior editor with *Money* magazine, it is a good idea for you to contribute to both a regular 401(k) and a Roth 401(k), if you can. If you are able to open both accounts, you can make decisions on what the best one is to put most of your money into, or you can keep the allocation even. But if you are young and plan to have more income later in life and, therefore, be in a higher tax bracket, you will want to put more money into the Roth 401(k). "Ditto," he wrote in the article, "if you are such a diligent saver that withdrawals from retirement accounts are likely to keep you in the same tax bracket as during your career, if not push you into a higher one." But, if you will for some reason fall into a lower tax bracket in retirement because you will not be earning that much from your retirement accounts and do not have a pension to collect, you will certainly want to put more money into your 401(k) account.

Roth 401(k)s and 403(b)s are new as of 2006. These accounts offer you the ability to contribute more than you can to a Roth IRA; however, these accounts are not available if your employer does not offer a normal 401(k) or 403(b) plan. There are no income limits placed on these accounts, and they follow 401(k) required minimum withdrawal rules. If you open one of these accounts and die, are disabled, or are over age 59 and a half, you are able to take a qualified distribution, which will not be taxed or penalized. You will also have the option to roll a Roth 401(k) or Roth 403(b) into a Roth IRA but not the other way around.

Self-Directed IRA

CASE STUDY: STEPHAN ROCHE
CEO, AMPLIO CORPORATION

Guidant Financial
13122 NE 20th Street, Suite 100
Bellevue, WA 98005
www.guidantfinancial.com
info@guidantfinancial.com
1-888-472-4455 – Voice
Stephan Roche, CEO, Amplio Corporation

Some of the benefits of a self-directed IRA are that you are invested in more diversified securities and are able to take advantage of the things you are more familiar with, giving you more control over your investments because you are guiding them directly. In addition, for some people, it allows them access to capital to do things they wanted to do but did not have the money to do before, like buying real estate. Some people just want to invest in a way where they can generate above-average returns, and in retirement and self-directed IRAs, that is the key. All the gains in a self-directed IRA are tax-deferred.

One of the drawbacks to a self-directed IRA is that you are in control of your retirement. You can make mistakes, and there is a risk to having this type of account. Of course, you should be generating higher returns because you are at a greater risk.

There is not ample awareness of self-directed IRAs. As we interview and survey people, the percentage who are aware of this type of retirement account is low. Even though the market of those looking for retirement accounts is quite large, this is not the right tool for everybody. Americans should only invest on a self-directed basis with eyes wide open, confidence in their investing ability, and a willingness to manage investments over time.

One of the drawbacks to a self-directed IRA is that you are in control. As with any investment, do your homework and go in with your eyes wide open, but believe in yourself, particularly if you are using the self-directed IRA to start a small business.

For these people, the self-directed IRA is an extraordinarily good option. In some respects, this is the safest capital you have

CASE STUDY: STEPHAN ROCHE
CEO, AMPLIO CORPORATION

access to in order to start a business, and you do not have to pay yourself back — there are no interest payments. This helps you to focus on the cash flow and on building your business. Many people say they would be more successful if they were able to focus on growing the business rather than paying back loans. But, as with all other investments, you have to be patient and have stamina. Investing is definitely a long-horizon activity, no matter where you invest.

In a low market, people who are invested in real estate for income-producing purposes do not need to sell, as long as they have rental income. Those that are investing today have many markets open to them. When someone comes to us with interest in a self-directed IRA, we have a conversation to determine whether they have an investment opportunity in mind, and we then make sure it is not prohibited by the IRS. And from their standpoint, there are several places in the country where investing in real estate will make an excellent transaction. Based on historical trends, as long as you hold it for at least seven years, you will make money.

Some of the biggest mistakes we see are made by people who are overconfident and believe they know more than they do. For other people, a big mistake is using 100 percent of their retirement funds to invest in a business. I do not know exactly what the right portion to use is, but you want to have some form of backup funds. Another mistake is not using a retirement fund. Many people think it is horrifying to use retirement funds to start a small business, but there are not many other good ways to finance a business. You could use your home equity, but if your business fails, now you cannot pay back your mortgage, and you risk defaulting. If you use a personal loan and your business fails, your credit score will be ruined if you cannot pay the loan back — and you will be bankrupt. If you use your traditional savings, you will have lost a considerable amount of money if your business fails — just as much as you would have lost in your retirement account, but now you will not have any savings to tap. Of course, you can lose your retirement account — that is a big deal and should not be underestimated. But if that happens, you go out, get a new job, and start putting money

CASE STUDY: STEPHAN ROCHE
CEO, AMPLIO CORPORATION

back into your account. You will not have any overhang, no one to pay back but yourself, so it is a reasonable road to take.

Fast Fact

There are no requirements to be in a self-directed IRA. Guidant Financial just evaluates your ability to be successful. They are not the fiduciary, so you operate independently. Typically, Guidant's customers already have a large sum saved in a retirement account and are, on average, wealthy, and have a high awareness level and sophistication about nontraditional investments. These people most often have high credit scores and are baby boomers.

Action Item

If your 401(k) plan does not offer a self-directed IRA option, ask for it. If you do not have a 401(k) or other retirement plan, just sign up for a self-directed IRA.

Automatic IRA

Currently, the AARP is working to push legislation through Congress that would create an automatic IRA. The automatic IRA would have deposits made through payroll deductions, much like a 401(k) account, and they would be put into a low-cost plan. The employee would be able to select an IRA for the deposits to go into, or an IRA would be selected for him or her if no choice is made. The investment options would have to be varied and would be partly based on the age of the person making the deposits into the account.

If the legislation passes, any employer with a company that has been open for more than ten years with ten or more employees would be asked to provide the automatic

IRA plan to employees. The benefit to employers would be a temporary tax credit for providing a savings option to employees and an additional credit for each employee that participates in the plan.

Fast Fact
A 2007 Prudential survey found that more than 80 percent of the businesses included in their survey felt that the automatic IRA would be good for their company.

CASE STUDY: ANDREW NANNIS, MEDIA RELATIONS; MANAGER LEO ESTRADA, AARP BOARD MEMBER

American Association of Retired People (AARP)
601 E Street, NW
Washington, DC 20049
www.aarp.org
asowens@aarp.org
1-888-OUR-AARP – Voice
1-202-434-6499 – Fax
Andrew Nannis, Media Relations
Manager Leo Estrada, AARP Board
Member (Senate testimony)

The push for the automatic IRA is AARP-specific. It is a piece of legislation that has bicameral support in the House and Senate. It would begin to close the gap between Americans who have the opportunity to save for retirement through their employers and those who do not. Approximately 50 percent do not have the opportunity to save for retirement at work.

From Leo Estrada's testimony before the Senate:

For many segments in the American population, the news about retirement savings is not good. "A third of Hispanics are no longer saving for retirement, and 26 percent are prematurely raiding their nest eggs to pay for everyday needs; half of all women have no pension; and 44.3 percent

CASE STUDY: ANDREW NANNIS, MEDIA RELATIONS; MANAGER LEO ESTRADA, AARP BOARD MEMBER

of African Americans age 65 and older receive all of their income from Social Security payments.

"According to the Internal Revenue Service, an estimated 79 million U.S. workers are not participating in a retirement plan in their workplace. Many of these workers are employed by businesses that do not even offer a retirement plan."

"The data also shows that only about 10 percent of people eligible to contribute to an IRA actually make contributions in any given year. As a result, a significant segment of the U.S. workforce does not save systematically for retirement."

"We are very pleased, Mr. Chairman, that you and the ranking member of the Subcommittee, Mr. English have introduced H.R. 2167, the Automatic IRA Act of 2007. We also appreciate the co-sponsorship of other Subcommittee members. The bipartisan support for this initiative is a positive development for our future retirement security."

"Your legislation proposes an ambitious but practical mechanism to expand retirement savings for millions of workers. This approach involves no employer contributions, no employer compliance with qualified plan or ERISA requirements, and no employer liability or responsibility for selecting a provider or opening IRAs for employees."

"According to an AARP survey, 84 percent of our members and 76 percent of Americans age 50 and older would like to have a workplace IRA."

"The lack of access to a workplace-based retirement savings plan is particularly acute for employees of small businesses. Only 44 percent of the employees who work in firms with less than 100 employees have access to an employer retirement plan. Employers currently can make payroll deduction IRAs available to their workers but clearly few do."

CASE STUDY: ANDREW NANNIS, MEDIA RELATIONS; MANAGER LEO ESTRADA, AARP BOARD MEMBER

"I will leave you with this final statistic. In a recent study on how the current economic downturn is affecting people, 74 percent said their elected officials are not doing enough to help those being squeezed by the current economy."

Retirement Accounts for the Self-Employed and Small Businesses

SEP and SEP IRA

Self-employed individuals have a few different retirement savings options available to them. They can open up Simplified Employee Pension plans (SEPs), which tend to be easier than a solo 401(k) to manage and contribute to. The SEP can be purchased from many different companies and has multiple investment choices, much like those of an IRA. Any contribution made to a SEP retirement account is tax-deductible. Self-employed individuals also have the option of opening up a solo 401(k) account. You are able to contribute more to a solo 401(k) than to a SEP account, and contributions are tax-deductible. To calculate how much you can contribute to a SEP, you take your business' income and subtract half of your self-employment tax from it, which should limit you to 20 percent of your business income. In 2007, this number went up to a maximum of $45,500. The contribution limit on a solo 401(k) will be reduced if you already donate to an employer-sponsored 401(k) through another job.

Individual 401(k)

Solo 401(k) accounts are best for the sole owner of a business who wants to maximize the contributions being made to a retirement plan. These accounts are not available for small businesses but rather, owner-only businesses. Known as the Individual 401(k), it is one of the newest options available to self-employed individuals for a retirement account. In a solo 401(k) account, you could contribute $45,500. Even though this maximum is the same as that of a SEP, you can, by and large, contribute more to a solo 401(k) because you can contribute up to $15,500 plus 20 percent of your business income (defined as your business income minus your self-employment tax).

Therefore, if you earn just $15,500 from self-employed work, you can contribute the full amount to a solo 401(k), while you can contribute only about $3,000 of that amount to a SEP. As with a traditional 401(k) account, the solo 401(k) allows you to play catch-up when you reach age 50 and contribute an extra $5,000 per year. Also, as with a 401(k) account, contributions grow tax-deferred, and you can take loans from the account if necessary. Unlike a 401(k), though, you can count any contribution made to a solo 401(k) as a tax write-off. If you are looking for an investment firm that offers solo 401(k) plans, you can find it at **www.401khelpcenter. com**. To be eligible to make contributions the following year, your account must be set up by December 31, and your first contribution must be made by April 15.

The Individual 401(k) was born out of the EGTRRA tax law in 2002 to give an incentive to small businesses where the owner is the sole employee or businesses where just the owner and his or her spouse are employees to set up 401(k) plans. One benefit of the Individual 401(k) is the ability for sole proprietors to make larger contributions to a 401(k) than they would be able to make to an IRA. In addition, tax-free loans are allowed up to 50 percent of the 401(k) up to a $50,000 maximum. When you pay back the interest on the loan, it goes right back into the Individual 401(k) account.

Individual 401(k) contribution limits in 2008 are $46,000 for those under age 50 and $51,000 for those 50 and older. This limit is made up of two parts — salary deferral and profit sharing. In 2008, for S or C corporations — or LLCs taxed as a corporation — the salary-deferral piece allows you to contribute 100 percent of W-2 earnings up to $15,500 (or $20,500 if age 50 or older), and profit sharing is capped at 25 percent of W-2 earnings. For sole proprietors, partners, or LLCs taxed as sole proprietors, the contribution is based on net adjusted business profit, which is gross self-employment income, minus business expenses, minus one half of the self-employment tax. In 2008, this meant 100 percent up to $15,500 ($10,500 if over age 50) and 20 percent of net adjusted business profits for profit sharing.

CASE STUDY: ERIC KUNIHOLM, PRINCIPAL

Beacon Capital Management Advisors
581 Boylston St., Suite 802
Boston, MA 02116
www.bcmadvisors.com
contact@bcmadvisors.com
1- 800-880-9833 – Voice
Eric Kuniholm, Principal

Since the EGTRRA law went into effect
in January 2002, Individual 401(k) plans started to become available, but people are still not knowledgeable about them. When the EGTRRA law passed and went into effect, it did not specifically create an Individual 401(k). What happened was when this law passed, it made a change that enabled a self-employed person to make a contribution to a retirement account as an employee and also created a profit-sharing piece to the account. A 401(k) used to be available if you were self-employed, but it did not offer any other benefits. So when this law was passed, you could make both employer and employee contributions, and the plan began to evolve. The federal government believes that it is simply an existing 401(k) plan, but it has now become advantageous for self-employed individuals.

The individual 401(k) is definitely underused. In the past, when self-employed individuals wanted to set up a retirement plan, the most popular choice was the SEP IRA — it was seen as a default option, and that was fine, but you can put more money into an individual 401(k), as long as you make less than $230,000 if you are a sole proprietor. This account is much better for the self-employed, especially because you are able to take out loans for your business tax-free and then you pay yourself back the interest, whereas with a normal 401(k) plan, you would have to pay taxes and penalties on the withdrawal, and you would be lucky to keep much of the original withdrawal amount.

Unlike with other retirement plans, no one is going to tell you about this one. It is all about you — you are the motivated person, you have the most to gain, so you need to do the research and figure it out. If you have a knowledgeable accountant, they might point you toward an Individual 401(k), but most of the time,

CASE STUDY: ERIC KUNIHOLM, PRINCIPAL

an individual just stumbles upon it. That is why Beacon does well in search engines because we want people to know about the Individual 401(k), so we set our site up to reflect that — we talk about how it works, why it is good, and what the benefits are.

Depending on who you get your Individual 401(k) account through, you will have different investment options. Some plans have many investment options — stocks, bonds, or mutual funds — some plans offer just one mutual fund family. And this can be good or bad for people because some want the ability to choose among many options, and others want to keep it simple.

The biggest drawback to an Individual 401(k) plan is that there is a little more paperwork to fill out, but that is minimal compared to the benefits. If you have $250,000 in assets, you have to fill out Form 5500, which is not a big deal and can usually be done by a financial company for cheap.

The employer contribution component is a big piece of the Individual 401(k) because as the employer, you get to choose how much you want to contribute to yourself in matching funds — and few employers are going to be as generous as you are and make the maximum allowed contribution. You would always choose to give yourself extra money for retirement unless you could not afford it.

Fast Fact

The Individual 401(k), as it is most commonly called, is otherwise known as an Individual(k), Solo 401(k), or Self Employed 401(k).

SIMPLE IRA

Another option for the self-employed is the Savings Incentive Match Plan for Employees IRA (SIMPLE IRA). This type of account is normally for small businesses, and much like any other retirement savings account, it takes a percentage or set dollar amount from your paycheck as contributions. The contribution limit is $6,000, but your employer (if you are using SIMPLE in a small business) is able to make matching contributions to your plan in one of two ways. Your employer can match dollar-for-dollar up to 3 percent of your pay or can make a fixed contribution of up to 2 percent of your pay. The nice thing about the SIMPLE IRA is that any employer-matching funds are immediately vested. You can keep your SIMPLE IRA if you should change jobs, and you are able to choose where your account funds are invested. To be eligible for a SIMPLE IRA, you must have made at least $5,000 from your employer during any two years prior to the year in which you plan to set up a SIMPLE IRA, and you must expect to make at least $5,000 during the calendar year in which you are making the contribution. Withdrawals follow the same rules as a traditional IRA. If you make an early withdrawal — before age 59 and a half — you will be responsible for paying a 10 percent early withdrawal penalty. There is, though, a two-year waiting period from the date you first enroll in your SIMPLE IRA plan until you can begin withdrawing funds. If you decide to withdraw before the two years is up, you will owe a 25 percent penalty.

Keogh

The Keogh plan is an option for small-business owners and self-employed individuals. It is commonly used as an incentive to encourage employees to stay with a company because the profit-sharing aspect of the Keogh plan offers a vesting schedule, which means the employees that stay the longest will reap the most benefits. This defined contribution plan is split into two different types: a pension plan and a money purchase plan. The pension plan lets employees choose how much they want to put into the account from year to year, while the money purchase plan requires the same percentage of income be put into the account each year. Employees are able to contribute the same amount to each type of account — to a maximum of $46,000 in 2008. Signing up to participate in either Keogh plan can be difficult and requires specific IRS documentation. If you do decide to sign up for this type of plan, your contributions will grow tax-deferred and will be tax-deductible.

CASE STUDY: ERIC KUNIHOLM, PRINCIPAL

ING DIRECT
ShareBuilder Advisors, LLC
1445 120th Ave NE
Bellevue, WA 98005
www.ingdirect.com
customercare@sharebuilder.com
1-866-747-2537 – Voice
Stuart Robertson, General Manager,
Principal

The employer and employee of a small business can save on taxes this year, save more for the long-term, and, ultimately, be rewarded for their efforts in helping the business succeed through matching and profit sharing. Consider that all participants, including the owner, receive:

- Higher contribution limits than a traditional IRA ($15,500 versus $5,000).

- Lower taxes via tax-deferred contributions in the calendar year plus tax-deferred savings for your retirement.

- Choose tax benefits of after-tax savings in the Roth 401(k)

CASE STUDY: ERIC KUNIHOLM, PRINCIPAL

- No income limits, and you can contribute up to $15,500 into it; company match must be done tax-deferred.

- Matching and profit sharing, if offered, are additional savings that are like free money or a bonus. The owner receives these too.

- In case of an emergency, you can choose to take a loan from your 401(k) plan of up to $50,000 without a tax hit, and you pay it back, interest and all, back to your 401(k) account. Beware, if you lose your job or leave your job, you will need to pay back the loan ASAP or you will be hit with taxes and a 10 percent penalty.

- Ability for employers to attract top talent via better benefits, which means more options for employees that want a small business environment with big business benefits.

- And you can expect a more loyal workforce and save the cost of replacing valuable employees. Nearly 40 percent of employees say they would leave their employer for a similar job just to get 401(k) benefits. The cost of replacing an employee ranges from 26 percent to 46 percent of a person's salary (that is $13,000 for a $50,000 position at 26 percent of salary).

Most small businesses have not taken the time to explore the benefits and accessibility of a 401(k) plan because of pre-conceived notions that they are too expensive and out of reach. Many also believe they need to have employees or that they cannot afford a match. First of all, you only need yourself — a sole proprietor can shelter $46,000 a year in a 401(k) plan. Second, matching is not required in a 401(k) plan, although it may limit how much you can contribute.

A few new online providers have focused on lowering costs and simplifying plan design and administration, so a plan requires minutes a month to manage. The government also helps by giving annual tax credits of $500 for the first three years of a new 401(k) plan (for a total of $1,500) to help offset administration costs. And if a company decides to match or do profit-sharing into the plan, these costs are typically, at least partially tax deductible, for the business.

CASE STUDY: ERIC KUNIHOLM, PRINCIPAL

If you are not offered a 401(k) by your employer, start and contribute to an IRA account, and at the same time, help your employer know how important a 401(k) benefit is to you and about new online providers that can make it easy to get a plan.

Benefits of a 401(k) for your business are many — long-term saving, lower taxes, access to cash, and government incentives — and it can help you keep your best employees. As for drawbacks, there are not many. While no small business likes more costs, $200 per year for a sole proprietor and $1,200 a year for a company of less than ten employees is money well spent. A 401(k) plan can provide a low-cost, big reward benefit, especially when compared to the larger out-of-pocket and growing costs of important benefits such as health care.

Fast Fact

The Web site, **www.ShareBuilder.com**, helps the general retail investor invest with low transaction costs, no account minimums, and helps put investing on autopilot. Even $50 a month can add up over the long haul. Stocks, bonds, and ETFs are the core offering. Folks can also choose mutual funds or, for more experienced investors, options.

Fast Fact

There is no real difference between the 401(k) offered by a small business and one offered by a large business. Large and small, 401(k) plans still have all the same tax advantages. To keep costs lower, the small business may not have the in-person contact, but rather, may manage the account online and over the phone. Given the advances in Internet technology with ease of use and video, it is a simple thing to do, without all the costs.

Chapter 12 Summary

- If you are not offered a retirement account at work or if you would like to supplement what you are offered, there are many options out there for you.

- IRAs and Roth IRAs are two options for people looking to supplement their income, and each has its own requirements and contribution limits (you must have an IRA before you can have a Roth IRA).

- For those who are self-employed or work for small businesses, SEPs, SEP IRAs, solo 401(k)s, SIMPLE IRAs, and Keoghs are available.

13

403(b) and 457 Plans

In this chapter, you will learn:

- What retirement options are available for those in the public sector

- How to take advantage of these plans

403(b) Plans

Another type of retirement savings plan that may be offered to you is the 403(b) plan. This type of retirement account is given mainly to people who are employed by hospitals, public schools, those who are clergy members, or anyone employed by a 501(c) (3) nonprofit organization. The 403(b) plan is similar to a 401(k), but your employer may not be as involved. Just like with a 401(k) plan, contributions will come straight out of your paycheck pre-tax, as long as you enroll in the plan. Any interest, contributions you make to the account, or employer-matching funds will grow tax-deferred until you begin making withdrawals.

The contribution limits in a 403(b) plan are the same as limits on 401(k)s. There are, though, special catch-up provisions. Some employees, such as those who work for public schools, hospitals, health and human service organizations, and churches, and who have at least 15 years of employment with their current employer can contribute an extra $3,000 per year, as long as they have not been contributing the maximum amount allowed in the past; this catch-up capped at $15,000. A complicated formula is used to determine how much you can contribute in catch-up dollars to your plan or if you are even eligible. The 403(b) plan also offers the over-50 catch-up that a 401(k) plan allows for, and you can play catch-up under both rules as long as you qualify. If you think you might be eligible for either catch-up program, ask your employer.

Investments are slightly different than in a 401(k) plan. Many employers only allow employees to invest in annuities, and in that realm, normally only variable annuities. (See Chapter 6 for more information, but essentially, these are mutual funds or mutual funds run by insurance companies, known as subaccounts. Variable annuities offer no guarantee on principal or gain on investment.) Stock and bond investments are never offered.

For the most part, withdrawals have the same restrictions as 401(k) plans, and hardship withdrawals and loans are often available (check with your employer about this). Be aware that if your money is in an annuity, you might need to pay an additional fee whether you make an early or on-time withdrawal. After you retire, if your 403(b) account funds are in an annuity, you will receive payments. Sometimes, you are able to receive a lump-sum payment, while other times, you need to take installments. On the other hand, if your money is in a mutual fund, you have many options for withdrawal upon your retirement (similar to those options in a 401(k) account that has invested in a mutual fund). If you began contributing money to a 403(b) plan before 1987, you can delay taking your withdrawals until you are 75.

Should you change employers while you hold a 403(b) account, you can, as of 2002, put that money into your new 401(k), 403(b), or 457 plan. You can even choose to roll it into an IRA of your choosing.

If your employer makes matching contributions to your plan, vesting rules are normally the same as those for 401(k) plans. Find out, before you sign up for your plan, exactly what the vesting rules are. Also, check-in occasionally to be sure that you are on track for full vesting at the appropriate date. Bear in mind that your employer or other plan administrator does make mistakes sometimes, so you need to be proactive in managing your account at all times.

As we talked about in Chapter 2, ERISA protects 401(k) plans and some 403(b) plans, but not all of them. Whether your plan is covered by ERISA is determined by how involved your employer is in the plan. In an ERISA-covered 403(b) plan, your employer makes decisions about the accounts held by his employees, including what you will be able to invest in. In a non-ERISA 403(b) account (mainly held by those working for public schools), your employer does not give much direction on where to invest your money. One benefit of the latter type of 403(b) plan is that you might be able to talk to your employer and get him or her to add the 403(b) provider you like most to the company's approved provider list. If you work for a church, your employer is not required to abide by ERISA rules and may offer a retirement income account that offers different investment opportunities.

CASE STUDY: 403(B) WISE

12067 Irish Mist Road NE
Albuquerque, NM 87122
http://403bwise.com
contactus@403bwise.com
Dan Otter, Owner-Operator, 403(b)wise

The 403(b) works much like a 401(k). It is a tax-deferred savings plan offered through an employer, whereas the 401(k) is most commonly offered by private-sector employers. Organizations eligible to offer a 403(b) are public schools, universities, and 501(c)(3) organizations.

403(b) plans do seem to be underused as it relates to K-12 plans, where estimates place participation at about two in five. This may have to do with the fact many school employees are automatically enrolled in pension plans. Another reason is the lack of both employer and employee understanding of the plan, and the acute lack of low-cost mutual funds.

In addition to only being open to schools and 501(c)(3) organizations, 403(b) participants are not able to invest directly in individual stocks. As I mentioned earlier, investment choices are often limited to higher fee insurance and brokerage products.

403(b) plans are beneficial because they are a supplement to pensions and offer the ability to save money on a tax-deferred basis.

The biggest mistake people make is failing to take advantage of this plan. This statement comes with a caveat — because of the lack of quality investment choices, some employees decline

CASE STUDY: 403(B) WISE

to invest in a 403(b) and either do not participate in a defined contribution (DC) plan, or invest instead in a Roth IRA.

The best advice is to find out how the plan works as soon as you are hired. And do not invest in any products until you understand basic investing principles and all the costs involved. If you are not happy with the investment choices you are offered, lobby your employer for better choices. Finally, focus on the long-term. Do not get caught up in daily, or even monthly, market fluctuations. Allocate based on your comfort level and life situation; rebalance as needed or, better yet, use a target date fund, and then, forget about it.

457 Plans

A 457 plan is considered deferred compensation, meaning money comes out of your paycheck and is given back to you at a set date, as in a 401(k) plan. This type of retirement account is most often offered to state and local government, and also some nonprofit employees. Many tax breaks are available to those who offer and hold 457 retirement accounts. The 457 account is split into two different parts — 457(b)s, which are like 401(k) plans, and 457(f)s, which are considered ineligible plans. You must be highly compensated to qualify for a 457(f). This type of account lets employees put off paying taxes, but you must agree to work for your company for a set amount of time.

Fast Fact

In a 457(b) plan, you are most often able to invest in mutual funds.

The contribution limits are the same as those governing 401(k) plans. Many 457(b) plans allow you to play catch-up if you are over age 50. If you are within three years of your plan's normal retirement age (note that police officers and firefighters who hold this plan are able to choose a retirement age that is lower than normal, but they are not able to retire before age 40), there is a bonus catch-up plan you can consider, which, if you qualify, lets you put double the normal allotted contribution into your account, if you have not contributed the maximum before. You can only participate in one each year, so if you qualify for both catch-up plans, pick the one that lets you contribute the most.

Your employer may offer a matching contribution plan, but it is unlikely. If your employer does offer matching contributions, or any other sort of contribution to your plan, the rules are different than in 401(k) plans, in that whatever your employer contributes will be added to your contribution and cannot exceed the contribution limit. To avoid this problem, some employers will put their contributions into a 401(a) account that is exactly like a 401(k) account, only you do not make contributions to it (but be aware that sometimes, you cannot control how money in a 401(a) is invested).

In the event that you are one of the lucky few who is offered multiple retirement savings options, you can, according to a 2001 law, contribute to a 457 and a 403(b) plan — and make maximum contributions to both.

When you decide to invest your funds, the rules are normally the same as with most other retirement plans. Your employer will offer a list of approved investments, and you will be able to choose among stocks, bonds, and mutual funds, just to name a few options.

Early withdrawals from a 457 plan are commonly more difficult than emergency withdrawals from a 401(k) plan. Be sure to ask your employer if you are able to make emergency withdrawals — and what constitutes an emergency. Most often, you may not be able to get money for a house or pay off higher education bills for yourself or your dependents. As with withdrawals in a 401(k) plan, you are required to begin making minimum withdrawals six months after you turn 70. Withdrawals are different from plan to plan. Some will allow you to take your money in installments, while others make you take it out all at once. Be sure to check with your employer on this one — if you are a bad saver, you most likely do not want to be stuck in a plan that forces you to make one lump-sum withdrawal when you reach retirement age.

If you change employers, you can take the money out of your account — of course, you will owe the required taxes, but there is no penalty. If you do not work for the government, but hold a 457 plan, you can roll that plan into a 401(k), 403(b), IRA, or another 457(b) plan. Yet, if you do work for the government, unless you roll over into another government-offered 457(b) plan, you will need to withdraw your money.

CASE STUDY: NATIONWIDE RETIREMENT SOLUTIONS

Nationwide Retirement Solutions
One Nationwide Plaza
Columbus, OH 43215
www.nrsforu.com
1-877-677-3678 – Voice
Matt Reibel, President
Nationwide Retirement Solutions

A 457 plan is the public-sector equivalent of a 401(k) plan. In more detail, what you have are two kinds of employer-sponsored retirement vehicles — classic defined benefit plans (pensions, where the employer is putting money in so the employee has a stream of income in retirement) and defined contribution plans (where the employee makes the determination about how much to invest in the account in order to have income in retirement). People who participate in 457 plans or public-sector defined contribution plans are normally people who work for states, cities, counties, and municipalities.

The normal 457 plan is known as a 457(b) plan and is for non-governmental, tax-exempt companies, excluding churches. The 457(f) plan is not eligible because it does not meet the requirements specified by the government. It covers executives and some employees who work for the government or other tax-exempt organizations. There are no contribution limits, and many plans are underfunded and can be taken by creditors in the event of a company filing for bankruptcy.

The Internal Revenue Code Section 457(g) requires 457(b) plan companies to keep any assets given to the fund by participants in a trust so that creditors cannot take that money if the company files for bankruptcy. Non-governmental, tax-exempt companies and 457(f) plans do not have to abide by this code.

Participation in 457 plans is typically used about half as much by public-sector employees as their private-sector counterparts. Average participation in a 457 plan is about 34 percent of all those eligible, whereas in a 401(k) plan, participation is more than double that — around 70 percent. The reason for this is that most public-sector employees have a fully defined benefit plan

CASE STUDY: NATIONWIDE RETIREMENT SOLUTIONS

intact, while the opposite is true of 401(k) plans in the private sector — few companies still offer new employees the classic defined benefit plan. People in the private sector know that their retirement will be based on their defined contribution plan, whereas in the public sector, employees know that is not necessarily true.

Fundamentally, there are not radical differences between a 401(k) and 457 plan as far as how you invest. Normally, the options as to where the money can be invested are similar. How you can receive your money at retirement is a little different. The major difference, which is really seen as an advantage, is that when someone separates from service (retires), they can start to draw money out of their 457 without penalty, no matter what age they are.

In a 457, the employer has fiduciary responsibility to make sure the plan is appropriate and has good investment options, which is one of the biggest protections offered by the plan. The money in a 457 plan is separate from a company's finances — it cannot be touched by creditors if an entity goes bankrupt.

The biggest benefits of 457s are the classic benefits that revolve around defined contribution plans to begin with. First, it is a forced savings program, so you make a decision as an employee to put a certain amount of money away, and that money comes right out of your paycheck and you never see it. Once an employee starts to do that, he or she almost does not think about it anymore, and builds a budget around the money he or she is getting after the retirement money is taken out of each paycheck. That is a great way to continue to invest on an ongoing basis. When the money comes out, it goes in tax-deferred; so if $100 goes into an employee's 457 account, it goes in before any taxes are taken out. When the money grows over time, it grows on a tax-deferred basis as well, until you begin taking the money out of the account. You have the benefit of not having to pay taxes up front, and your account can grow bigger over time because of compounding interest on a larger amount.

It is a good thing that we are all living longer. But the bad thing is that we are all living longer. This means that when someone retires now, they need more money for a longer life expectancy.

CASE STUDY: NATIONWIDE RETIREMENT SOLUTIONS

What makes it more challenging for the public sector is that many people retire earlier, so that makes the time even longer. Healthcare costs are also rising at a much faster rate than inflation or anything along those lines, so if you live longer and have higher healthcare costs, suddenly you need to be saving and investing considerable money. So, save early, save often, save consistently, and save plenty.

Older investors should know that it is never too late to start saving. Many people get to a point where they think there is no point to saving, and they do not realize that there is always value, no matter how close someone is to retirement. There is always value to putting money away and letting it work for you — especially when you can take advantage of catch-up contributions.

Start saving as early as you can, and be consistent. The defined contribution 457 plan is different from a defined benefit plan because someone else is not investing the money for you. Sit down with one of your retirement plan representatives and make sure you are taking into consideration how long you have to invest and what your risk tolerance is, and develop a portfolio that matches up with that. That is the first thing — making sure you have a well-diversified investment strategy and then sticking with it by taking a long-term perspective. The economy has all sorts of ups and downs, but even though these happen, the overall trend is still up. Do not get nervous; stay with your strategy. Based on historical trends, the market will come back up.

There are two big mistakes investors make; one is not starting to contribute to a retirement account early enough. There is the whole idea of compounding interest, how often your money doubles. The best friend an employee can ever have is time when you are investing. The other mistake is not putting enough in. Contribute as much to the account as you can. Sometimes, people stop contributing and never start again, or they take money out of their retirement account before they are ready to retire through a loan or hardship withdrawal, and these things take away the advantage of saving.

A big piece of advice is to save early and save often. Even

CASE STUDY: NATIONWIDE RETIREMENT SOLUTIONS

though the public sector traditionally has healthy pensions, in most cases, that will not be enough for people to retire on. They need to supplement their income. It is a common mistake to think that pension and Social Security will be enough.

Rebalancing has much to do with personal preference — some people like to look every quarter, which is fine, because you should be more involved, rather than less involved. But if you look in once per year and make any necessary adjustments, that should be fine. This brings to the forefront one of the mistakes people make in that they do not make the right diversification or asset allocation decisions at the beginning, so they have a poorly diversified portfolio from the start. The other thing that happens is they set it and forget it. People need to make sure they get the right investment mix at the beginning and think about how they can stay on top of that to make sure they are invested the way they want to be. This whole situation calls out for managed accounts, which is one of the most valuable things that have come into the retirement market lately. A managed account can be useful, as long as you ensure that the account is OK up front and stays appropriate for you over time, ensuring proper diversification. Managed accounts tend to allow people to do this easily.

In the public sector, there is not much investment switching, and that is true of most defined contribution plans in general. The 401(k) statistics show that people make a decision about how they want to invest, and 70 percent never make a change, ever, from their original decision. Part of this is caused by the payroll deduction factor, which involves little change and takes advantage of dollar-cost averaging in which you invest when the market is up and when it is down. There are not many people jumping ship right now. Many more people than normal, however, are taking money out through hardship withdrawals or loans, and that is all driven by a tough economy — people get into tough situations, so they feel they need to tap into their retirement plans. What happens to our company is that people do not move money around, but when funny things happen in the market, their service centers get quite busy, so we provide education and perspective. Plenty of hand holding goes on just to reassure people.

CASE STUDY: NATIONWIDE RETIREMENT SOLUTIONS

In general, when government workers make investments, they are more conservative from the beginning than their private-sector counterparts. So that may be why you do not see as much movement in terms of investments, because they have always been overly conservative with how the money has been allocated.

Chapter 13 Summary

- Those who work in the public sector or who work for nonprofit organizations are unlikely to be offered 401(k) accounts, but will instead have 403(b) or 457 plans.

- 403(b) accounts are much like 401(k) accounts, and tend to be underused.

- 457s are generally offered to those working in state and local government, and the most common type of investment offered is mutual funds.

14 *Mistakes to Avoid and Questions to Ask*

There are two things that are crucial to ensuring that you properly manage your 401(k) account and ensure the best possible retirement for yourself. First, know how much you want and how much you will actually need in retirement (there is a difference — be sure to have a realistic goal, or even one that is lower than what you plan to end up with, and a goal that you can truly work for). The number you come up with will affect what you do with your account from the time you begin investing until you are no longer able to put money into the account. If you do not have a plan for retirement, you will have nothing to work for. Second, you should pay careful attention to your asset allocation. This means that you should decide what percentage of your 401(k) account you want to put into stocks and what percentage you put into bonds. Be sure to plan according to your age, what you want to do in retirement, and how your investments have been performing thus far.

Questions to Ask

1. Am I eligible to participate in a 401(k) plan?

2. When can I begin participating in your 401(k) plan?

3. Is participation mandatory? If so, will you automatically enroll me?

4. How do I enroll?

5. If I do not elect to open a 401(k) account when I am first eligible, can I start at a later date?

6. How and when can I change the amount I contribute?

7. Is there an employer-matching program? If so, how much will you contribute to my plan? Do I have to make a certain contribution to my own account to be eligible to receive it?

8. Do you offer any other forms of retirement plans that I can enroll in as a substitute for or in addition to my 401(k) plan?

9. How much do I need to set aside to have enough money to sustain my current lifestyle in retirement? How much will I need to live large?

10. How often can I or should I reallocate my investments?

11. What happens to my 401(k) or other retirement account if I change employers?

12. If I choose to retire early, what will happen to my 401(k) funds? Will any fees be imposed on me?

13. What is the maximum amount I can contribute to my 401(k) or other retirement account, per employer rules?

14. What is the maximum amount I can contribute to my 401(k) or other retirement account, per federal rules?

15. If I had a 401(k) or other retirement account with another employer, can I roll that amount into my new account?

16. When will I be fully vested? What is the vesting schedule?

17. What investment options are available to me?

18. Whom should I go to when I have questions about my account?

19. How do I manage my account?

20. Can I make any early withdrawals? If so, under what conditions? And what penalties and taxes will be charged to me?

21. How can I choose or change my beneficiary? Up until what point am I able to change my beneficiary?

22. At what age must I cease making contributions to my 401(k) account?

23. Are there required minimum distributions? When must I begin taking them, and how much must I take at each withdrawal?

24. Who can give me advice on my investment options?

25. How often will I be given information regarding my account and its performance?

26. What fees, if any, will I be responsible for paying?

27. How long will it be before I need to make withdrawals?

28. How much risk can I tolerate?

29. How are withdrawals paid to me? Do I have multiple options?

Mistakes to Avoid

A Tip from ShareBuilder

Three Major Mistakes

1. Not participating in a 401(k) plan — especially among younger employees. The impact on their savings and hitting their goals can be much easier just because they started young (the power of compounding). Just investing a little now can go a long way for tomorrow. By not participating, folks often are passing on "free" money of a company match.

2. Most investors do a poor job of asset allocation — choosing how to invest your money across stocks, bonds, and cash. Research studies continually show asset allocation as the most important variable in how your savings will grow over time. It is why we encourage participants to choose from one of our five model portfolios (from conservative to aggressive) to help make it easy for participants to make a smart decision and get on track to meet their goals.

It is important to remember that planning for your future is not something you can do on a whim one weekend. It takes time and patience to grow your nest egg, if you plan to retire rich, and there is much to know and think about. To make matters a little easier, the following are some mistakes to avoid. If you do not do anything else, just avoid these actions:

A Tip from ShareBuilder

1. Not doing your research on investment options. You do not need to be a genius to invest your retirement account dollars, but you do need to do a little research on how the investments have performed in the past, whom they are held by, and whether they fit into your long-term investment plan.

2. Not investing in your 401(k) or any retirement plan that is offered to you.

3. Not checking in on your investments to see how they are performing and reallocating your investments as necessary. Reallocation is essential, especially as you age and your life situations change.

4. Being too risky in your investments. Too much risk can be especially detrimental when you are closer to retirement because if the market takes a big dip, your retirement funds will be hit hard.

5. Being too conservative in your investments. If you decide not to take on any risk, you will be hurting yourself because your account will not be able to grow or keep up with the rate of inflation, meaning you will have little more than your initial investments once you retire.

6. Not designating a beneficiary or not updating your beneficiary as circumstances change. Your spouse is automatically your beneficiary upon your death (whether you are estranged or not), unless he or she signs a waiver.

7. Making unnecessary early withdrawals.

8. Contributing too much. Do not make yourself live in poverty during your working years just so you can be rich in retirement.

9. Contributing too little. Be sure that you have a long-term retirement plan and that you stick to it. Do not have unrealistic hopes if you are not going to contribute enough to your account while you are working. You also want to be sure that you are taking full advantage of any matching funds your employer offers.

A Tip from ShareBuilder

10. Not rolling over your retirement account to a new employer or to an IRA. If you leave your retirement account with your old employer, you will not have any input into what investments are offered, and you may be limited as to how often you can reallocate your funds or what you can invest in.

11. Accepting a check from your employer for transfer into an IRA or new 401(k) account rather than having the money rolled over directly — your employer will have to withhold 20 percent for taxes, and you will have to put the money into an IRA yourself within 60 days, including the 20 percent your employer did not give you (this will have to come out of your own pocket). If even a single penny goes missing from that check, you will be taxed and subjected to an early withdrawal penalty.

12. Holding too much stock in large companies and not enough stock in smaller companies, which have historically outperformed the stock of larger companies.

13. Not investing in international companies.

14. Believing that an investment's past performance will indicate its future performance. It is not worth going after what was hot last year, because even though it can be irritating to see a stock or bond you did not pick grow to large numbers, it could easily be the worst-performing stock or bond in the year ahead. In addition, if you switch your investments every single year, or more frequently than that, you will miss out on the potential growth of your investment or on gaining back what you lost. If you constantly switch investments, you are opening yourself up to a ton of risk.

15. Buying too much company stock. This can be a mistake because you are relying on your employer for paycheck while you are in the workforce as well as money while you are in retirement. You do not want to be completely dependent on one place. There is too much risk involved in this, especially if you end up being fired or laid off. According to CNN, "Some 42 percent of 401(k) assets at large companies are vulnerable in this way." You are not being loyal; you are just putting your retirement future at risk.

A Tip from ShareBuilder

16. Not choosing to invest in stocks. Many people think that entering the stock market is too much work and not worth the risk, especially now when the markets look so bad. These people often throw their money into investments that will not even keep up with the rate of inflation. Take the risk and invest in stocks — larger companies are more stable, and smaller companies often have nowhere to go but up.

17. Not taking full advantage of matching funds. Always be sure to contribute enough to your account to ensure that you are taking full advantage of what your employer is giving away.

18. Being overly confident in your investment choices, especially if you choose nontraditional investments like real estate or opening a small business.

15
Conclusion

There is a whole world that opens up to you when you make a plan for retirement and stick to it. And with the many investment options and help offered by employers, there is no reason for you not to save for some of the best years of your life. The most important thing to remember is that retirement planning is a long-term commitment — it should not be entered into too quickly, and you certainly should not get out of it the first time things start to go wrong. The longer you remain in the retirement market, the better off you will be when you finally do leave your job and buy that new house, travel the world, spend time with your grandchildren, or do whatever you plan to do once you retire. Be willing to adjust to whatever comes your way.

Right now, the market is extremely turbulent, but that does not mean you should stop making contributions to your 401(k) or other retirement account, or that you should begin making early withdrawals. This is not the time to start pulling your money out of the higher-risk investments you currently hold and putting it into lower risk investments — you do not want to sell low. A poor economy can be scary, especially when you are older, but do not panic, as it will only harm you more. Just keep focused on your long-term goal — a more-than-comfortable retirement.

In October 1987, the stock market dropped 23 percent. Between 2000 and 2002, it dropped 47 percent, and after Sept. 11, it dropped 684 points. The important thing to learn from this is that every time the market dropped, it rebounded. Also, according to Ibbotson Associates, since 1926, stocks of large companies annually return over 10 percent. When the market is substantially down — that is, when you have the best chance to make the biggest gains — you can buy low and stand to make big gains when the market finally does rebound. Right now is the perfect time to check how comfortable you actually are with your investments and analyze your current plan. If you stop investing now, you will miss out on interest and any matching contributions your employer offers.

If you can, it is a good idea to open multiple retirement accounts so you are able to put away as much money as possible for your retirement. Carefully keep track of each of your accounts and all your required start dates and required minimum distributions. You do not want to be hit with a 50 percent penalty for missing one.

Life insurance is something you should consider that was not mentioned in this book. It is good for obvious reasons, but it can also help offset any income or estate taxes your beneficiaries will need to pay on your retirement account. If you decide to get life insurance, you will want to be sure to cover necessary expenses for those you leave behind and the taxes that will need to be covered on your retirement plan. In addition to this, it is always a good idea to know who the income taxes on any retirement accounts you have will be cheaper for — you or your beneficiaries. Figuring this out might make a difference as to when you are planning to take withdrawals and how much you will take.

Whatever you do, remember the basic goals of saving for retirement: begin saving early, have a retirement goal in mind, save as much as you can, invest wisely, reallocate when necessary, be in it for the long-term, and enjoy your retirement. With the wealth of information out there on 401(k) plans, you, too, can retire rich and enjoy your non-working years.

CASE STUDY: THE NERVOUS RETIREE

By Robert J. Phillips
Chief Retirement Consultant for
www.retirementcalc.com
Used with permission:
www.retirementcalc.com

Like most of you, during my working years, I planned and saved for a comfortable retirement. There is no shortage of resources available to help with retirement planning. Numerous books, financial institutions, and consultants are available, and calculators can be used to determine how much you have to save to have a comfortable retirement.

I have found that most retirees who took an interest in retirement planning did a good job in implementing their retirement savings plans. They take great pride in their accomplishment.

The problem comes after you have retired. Something happens psychologically to retirees. They have a difficult time transitioning from an aggressive saver to an active spender. In other words, it is hard to change that savings account into a spending account. They see the savings as a trophy, the culmination of a lifelong

CASE STUDY: THE NERVOUS RETIREE

goal. Their entire working life has been a savings culture, now they must change their thinking to using their investments as a resource for retirement income.

Even more important, a major market downturn like the one we just recently experienced makes them extremely nervous. Many have seen their entire savings drop by 40 percent. They worry that if they start to spend their money during a major market downturn, the money will not last. Just at the time they should be enjoying the fruit of their long years of saving, they abandon the plan.

Many retirees are afraid to tap into their savings. Some even plan to go back to work in order to survive. Many will restrict their withdrawals and shift their assets to more secure fixed income investments, including the money market.

Others will turn their money over to a financial manager or put the money in an annuity for safety. The cost for such services is typically 2 percent of the money invested. If you are trying to achieve an 8 percent return on your investments, this cost can represent 25 percent of the income you can produce from these investments. All of these actions by retirees reduce their available income at a time they should be fully enjoying the income that their savings can produce.

This is increasingly important for future retirees. Baby Boomers will likely have most of their retirement income coming from self-managed accounts.

Companies are eliminating funded pension plans in favor of self-managed accounts. In addition, these companies are reducing or eliminating health care coverage for retirees, which will further strain a retiree's income needs. Also, the future of Social Security is in doubt. The bottom line is that future retirees will need to actively manage their accounts while maximizing their returns in order to enjoy a comfortable life style.

Action Item

Do not take retirement on a whim — take time to calculate whether you have enough money to leave the workforce when you plan to and have an alternate strategy.

Action Item

Review your goals periodically to see whether you are still able to meet them or if you will be able to overcome them sooner than expected — also check in on your spending habits.

Action Item

Educate yourself.

401(k): A 401(k) plan is an employer-sponsored retirement fund that allows any participants to contribute money from their salary in a tax-deferred fashion.

403(b) plan: A tax-sheltered annuity offered to tax-exempt employees (including those who work for the public school system). The employer may defer taxes on his or her contribution.

Actual Deferral Percentage: A test that looks at how much of a paycheck is deferred to a retirement plan for highly compensated employees versus how much is contributed by non-highly compensated employees.

Adjusted gross income (AGI): Your total income (before taxes) minus any adjustments to your income.

After-tax: Any contributions made to your retirement account that are deducted from your paycheck after taxes have been taken out.

American Stock Exchange (AMEX): Trades only small- to mid-sized stocks in addition to options and exchange-traded funds.

Annuities: Regular payments from a

retirement account or insurance company that holds your annuity contract.

Asset class: Securities that behave similarly on the market and share similar characteristics. There are three major types: equities (stocks), fixed-income (bonds), and cash equivalents (money market funds).

Automatic Enrollment: An employer-sponsored plan that automatically opens a retirement savings account for eligible employees. The employee does not need to sign up for this plan and can opt out from contributing any money by submitting a form to human resources.

Bear market: Stock prices are down significantly.

Beneficiary: The person, persons, or fund that will receive the money in your 401(k) or other retirement account in the event of your death.

Beta: The risk of a single investment compared to the risk of the market as a whole.

Blue-chip stocks: A stable investment because the companies considered blue-chip are normally older and have established themselves in the market. All stocks listed in the Dow Jones Industrial Average fall into this category.

Brokerage window: May be offered by your employer; it lets you invest in things outside of what is offered by your company (otherwise known as a self-directed option). This often comes at an extra fee, and you should be careful if you have one. Often, people believe they can use the brokerage window for day trading, but not many use it successfully to make quick money (this is also the reason why many employers do not offer this option).

Bull market: Stock prices rise significantly.

Cafeteria plan: A benefit plan offering a choice from a menu of cash or two or more benefits.

Cash or deferred arrangement (CODA): A 401(k) plan or similar retirement plan where an employee is able to make contributions to an employer-offered account.

Cash profit-sharing plan: A type of profit-sharing or stock bonus plan in which employees may defer current compensation on a pre-tax basis.

Certificate of Deposit (CD): Offered by a bank, but unlike a bank account, you are required to leave your money in the CD for a set amount of time. At the end of that term, you will receive your initial investment plus an interest rate that was guaranteed at the start of the CD's term. Often, this interest rate is higher than that of a savings account.

Compensation: What you earn from working (including tips and bonuses, for example).

Compounding: Earning interest on your interest (another benefit of a long-term investment).

Defined benefit plans: A retirement plan sponsored by your employer. Investments are controlled by your employer, and benefits are divvied out using a formula that includes salary history and how long you have been with your employer. May also be known as qualified benefit plans and non-qualified benefit plans.

Defined contribution plans: A retirement plan in which your employer sets aside a certain amount of money each year for your retirement.

Department of Labor: A federal agency that helps to ensure that workers across the country have adequate working conditions, pay, opportunities for employment, benefits, and other entitlements. They ensure that collective bargaining can take place and administer laws regarding wages, discrimination, unemployment, and safe working conditions.

Determination letter: A document from the IRS that states that a retirement plan meets IRS requirements for tax-advantaged treatment.

Direct transfer: A tax-free transfer of retirement savings funds from one account sponsor to another (for example, taking your 401(k) account with you to another employer).

Disclosure: The release of all information about a company that can influence a decision about investing in it.

Distribution: A payment from your retirement account — can come in installments or one lump sum.

Dollar-cost averaging: Deducting the same amount from your paycheck each month, which means you do not have to worry as much about the fluctuating markets — you will constantly be spending the same amount each month so that sometimes you buy high and sometimes you buy low.

Early withdrawal penalty: For 401(k) accounts, any money withdrawn before you reach age 59 and a half is subject to a 10 percent penalty.

Eligibility: Your ability to participate in your employer's retirement plan.

Employee Benefits Security Administration: A division of the Department of Labor that protects benefits given to employees by their employers, and helps workers understand and receive necessary information on any benefits they are eligible for through their employers.

Employee Retirement Income Security Act (ERISA): Sets minimum standards employers must follow if they offer retirement plans, health plans, or pensions to their employees and former employees.

Employee Stock Ownership Plan (ESOP): In an employee stock ownership plan, the employer gives company stock to employees.

Employees do not buy or hold the stock.

Employee Stock Option Plan: The ability of an employee to purchase stock from the company he or she works for at a set price over a certain amount of time.

Equities: A security that represents ownership in a company (for example, stocks).

ESOP: Employee Stock Option Plan.

ESPP: Employee Stock Purchase Plan.

Excess Aggregate Contributions: Contributions made after tax, or employer-matching contributions, that cause a company to fail the IRS's actual contribution percentage test.

Facts and circumstances test: A test used to determine whether you are able to make a hardship withdrawal.

Fidelity bond: If the fiduciary or anyone else responsible for your plan steals any of the funds or does not make investments the way you asked, the fiduciary bond will protect you.

Fiduciary: The person with the responsibility for making financial choices regarding your retirement account that benefit you and others in your plan rather than him- or herself and your company, for example.

Fiduciary responsibility: Anyone with a decision-making role in your 401(k) plan's investments is legally bound to make those decisions in the best interests of the plan participants (you and your coworkers), not in the best interest of the company, the plan provider, or anyone else. This person can be sued if he or she does not do what is required.

Form 1099R: A form indicating the amount you received in a distribution that is filed with the IRS.

Form 5500: All qualified plans — except for SEPs and SIMPLE IRAs — must file this form yearly with the IRS.

Full retirement age: Full retirement age is currently 65 for those born before 1938, and the age gradually increases until it reaches 67 for those born after 1959.

Growth stocks: Stocks that have a perceived potential for high capital appreciation, equating to higher earnings for stockholders.

Guaranteed Investment Contracts (GIC): An investment that returns a fixed rate and is held through an insurance company.

Hardship withdrawal: An early withdrawal made from a retirement account that occurs when the account holder experiences proven financial hardship. Penalties and taxes are applied to this type of withdrawal.

Highly compensated employee: An employee who owns more than 5 percent of the company they work for, or, for the previous year, earned more than $100,000 (if this is 2008; $105,000 if the year is 2009). Highly compensated employees have restrictions placed on them by the IRS as to how much they can contribute to a 401(k) plan so as to keep it fair for everyone.

Income stocks: Low- to moderate-risk stocks, often held in stable industries, such as telecommunications or utilities.

Inflation: The rise in prices of goods and services over time.

Internal Revenue Service (IRS): The arm of the U.S. Treasury that is responsible for administering retirement plan and pension rules.

Keogh Plan: Allows self-employed people to contribute to a retirement account that is a defined contribution.

KSOP: A plan with 401(k) contributions and an employee stock plan.

Large-cap stocks: Market capitalization higher than $10 billion.

Lump sum distribution: Receiving one payment for all the money in your retirement plan.

Market capitalization: The value of a company determined by the market price of its outstanding stock and the number of stocks it has outstanding.

Matching contribution: A contribution made by the retirement account holder's employer into the account, by and large, as a percentage of what the employee contributes to his or her retirement account or a percentage of the employee's pay.

Mid-cap stocks: Market capitalization between $2 billion and $10 billion.

Money market fund: A mutual fund with holdings in short-term securities.

Monte Carlo Analysis: Repeated random sampling done through the use of computer analytics.

Multiemployer plan: Using collective bargaining agreements, this plan is contributed to by two or more employers.

Mutual fund: An investment that pools together money from multiple investors to be able to invest in different securities, such as stocks, bonds, money market funds, and other asset classes. The fund manager invests the money in a way that ensures the fund is working to produce capital gains for those invested. A prospectus details how your mutual funds are performing. Mutual funds are especially helpful for investors putting less money into the account because it allows them to get a hold of professionally managed funds without having to pay high fees or invest vast amounts of money. In a mutual fund, each investor shares proportionally in the buying and selling of investments as well as the performance of each investment.

National Association of Securities Dealers Automated Quotation System (NASDAQ): The largest of the U.S. stock markets; it makes the most trades per day and has more than 3,200 companies listed on it.

New York Stock Exchange (NYSE): By dollar volume, this is considered the largest stock exchange in the world. In terms of the companies listed on this market, it falls second in the world only to NASDAQ.

Non-Highly compensated employee: Employees who earn less than $105,000 in 2008.

Nonqualified plan: A retirement plan in which the premiums are not tax-deductible.

Non-tax-deductible: Something that you cannot use to reduce your taxable income (like contributions to a Roth IRA).

Pension: A classic defined benefit plan in which the employer makes contributions to a fund and invests the money on behalf of the employee so that he or she will receive benefits from this fund in retirement. Unlike a defined contribution plan, in a defined benefit plan, an employee never makes contributions to the fund.

Plan administrator: Monitors the day-to-day activities of a 401(k) plan.

Plan sponsor: The person who sets up a company's retirement plan and determines who may participate, what the investment options will be, and can make matching contribution payments.

Plan year: Twelve months, calculated by calendar years, fiscal years, or another measure.

Pre-tax: Any contributions made to your retirement account that are deducted before taxes are taking from your paycheck.

Price/book ratio: An equation that compares

a stock's market value to its book price. Calculated by dividing stock price by total assets.

Price/earnings ratio: Market value per share divided by earnings per share.

Profit sharing plan: A program through which an employer shares the company's profits with the company's employees. Normally, the amount an employee receives is based on a percentage of the profits, the employee's salary, and his or her time with the company.

Qualified Domestic Relations Order (QDRO): A court order that says you must give all or a part of your retirement account to whoever is named — such as your husband, wife, or child.

Qualified Joint and Survivor Annuity (QJSA): An annuity in which, upon your death, the payments automatically roll over to your spouse and are equal to at least 50 percent of what you were receiving.

Qualified plan: A retirement plan that allows interest to grow tax-free or tax-deferred.

Recharacterization: Treating a contribution to an IRA plan like it was contributed to another IRA and not the one initially contributed to.

Required minimum distributions (RMD): The IRS requires that you begin making withdrawals from your 401(k) account when you turn 70 and a half. You must make withdrawals each year after that. The amount you must withdraw is based on your account balance and life expectancy.

Rollover: Moving investments from one retirement account to another.

Roth 401(k): A retirement savings account combining the benefits of the Roth IRA account with those of the 401(k) account.

Roth IRA: A retirement savings plan directed to high-income earners who are unable to participate in employer-sponsored retirement plans. The contributions made to the fund grow tax-free and withdrawals are tax-free as long as the account holder meets certain criteria. Contributions are not tax-deductible.

Safe Harbor Rules: Allow some people or companies to be exempt from regulations.

Schedule SSA: A form filed with the federal government that deals with vesting status.

Salary deferral: A form from your employer stating how much you elect to set aside from your pre-tax salary and put into your retirement account.

Securities: The multitude of investments offered including stocks, bonds, and mutual funds, just to name a few.

Savings Incentive Match Plan for Employees IRA (SIMPLE IRA): A savings option for the self-employed. This type of account is normally for small businesses, and it takes a percentage or set dollar amount from the employee's paycheck as contributions.

Small-cap stocks: Market capitalization between $300 million and $2 billion.

Stock Bonus Plan: Defined contribution plan with matching contributions made through company stock.

Summary Plan Description: A document detailing a retirement plan, including who is able to participate in the plan.

Target benefit plan: Similar to a defined benefit plan, but the benefits cannot be guaranteed because they are based on the performance of the fund's investments.

Tax deductible: Something that can reduce your taxable income.

Top-heavy plan: A retirement plan that benefits highly compensated employees or owners of the company.

Traditional IRA: A retirement account in which contributions can be either tax-deductible or non-tax-deductible. Any interest in the account grows tax-deferred and withdrawals are taxable, unless the withdrawal comes from the non-tax-deductible portion of the account.

Trustee: A bank or investment company with fiduciary responsibility who acts in the stead of your employer to upkeep and monitor your 401(k) account.

Vesting: A time period after which the employee receives the rights to employer contributions to his or her 401(k) plan.

Vesting schedule: The time in which an employee becomes fully vested in the employer contributions offered by his or her retirement plan.

Appendix B

Additional Resources

www.choosetosave.org/ballpark/ballparkWorksheet-2005final.pdf
www.stretcher.com/stories/980112a.cfm
www.socialsecurity.gov
www.irs.gov
Withdrawals: www.irs.gov/retirement/article/0,,id=162416,00.html
IRS PUBLICATION 590: www.irs.gov/pub/irs-pdf/p590.pdf
www.moneycentral.msn.com/retire/planner.aspx
www.mpowercafe.com
www.403bwise.com
www.457wise.com
www.bankrate.com
IRS PUBLICATION 571: www.irs.gov/pub/irs-pdf/p571.pdf
INSURANCE COMPANY RATINGS: www.insure.com/articles/interactivetools/sandp/newtool1.jsp

NASDAQ: **www.nasdaq.com**
NYSE: **www.nyse.com**
AMEX: **www.amex.com**
Retirement income calculator: **www.moneycentral.msn.com/investor/calcs/n_retire/main.asp**
Retirement expense calculator: **www.moneycentral.msn.com/investor/calcs/n_retireq/main.asp**
Mutual fund cost calculator: **www.sec.gov/investor/tools.shtml**
Social Security Administration: **www.socialsecurity.gov**
Investment dictionary: **www.investopedia.com**
Investment Company Institute: **www.ici.org**
Expense and growth calculator: **www.tiaa-cref.org/calcs/expensegrowth/index.html**
Retirement goal calculator: **www3.tiaa-cref.org/reteval/RetServlet**
www.401khelpcenter.com
www.finra.org
Assistance for those 50 and older interested in opening their own business: **www.bizstarters.com**
For a list of solo 401(k) account providers: **www.401khelpcenter.com**
MetLife offers investment and 401(k) advice: **www.lifeadvice.com**
The Mutual Fund Education Alliance: **www.mfea.com**
Fidelity Investments: **www.fidelity.com**
Vanguard: **www.vanguard.com**

The Wall Street Journal's personal finance magazine, *SmartMoney*: **www.smartmoney.com**
CNN's financial network and Web site: **www.cnnfn.com**
Scudder Kemper Investments: **www.scudder.com**
T. Rowe Price Associates: **www.troweprice.com**
American Century Investments: **www.americancentury.com**
A life expectancy calculator: **www.livingto100.com**
www.coffeehouseinvestor.com
www.bylo.org
www.analyzenow.com
www.fundadvice.com
www.rightonthemoney.com
Forbes
Business Week
Money
The Wall Street Journal
Barron's
Fortune
Kiplinger's
Plan Sponsor Magazine
Bloomberg Personal Finance
CBS Market Watch

CNBC News
"When the Good Pensions Go Away: Why America Needs a New Deal for Pension and Healthcare Reform": Thomas Mackell offers ideas on how to fix the problems plaguing the healthcare and pension systems.

Profit Sharing/401(k) Council of America

20 N. Wacker Drive, Suite 3700

Chicago, IL 60606

Phone: 312-419-1863

Email: psca@psca.org

www.psca.org

Department of Labor

Frances Perkins Building

200 Constitution Ave., NW

Washington, DC 20210

Phone: 1-866-4-USA-DOL

www.dol.gov

Internal Revenue Service

Phone help service: 1-800-829-1040

www.irs.gov

Appendix C

Life
Expectancy

Fast Fact
According to the Health and Retirement Study, in 1950, a 65-year-old man could expect to live another 13 years, while a woman could expect to live an extra 15 years. Today, that number has risen to 17 years for men and 20 years for women.

Fast Fact
Women, on average, live longer than men.

Retirement Myth
With advances in science and medicine, there is no telling how long I will live: It is true that we are living longer, and it is also true that it is hard to estimate what birthday you will make it to. See the following life expectancy table — people generally do not make it to see their 100th birthday, but that does not mean you should not plan like you are going to.

LIFE EXPECTANCY TABLE	
Current Age	**Life Expectancy (years remaining)**
From the IRS Publication 590, 2007	
http://www.irs.gov/pub/irs-pdf/p590.pdf	
25	58.2 years

LIFE EXPECTANCY TABLE	
Current Age	**Life Expectancy (years remaining)**
26	57.2 years
27	56.2 years
28	55.3 years
29	54.3 years
30	53.3 years
31	52.4 years
32	51.4 years
33	50.4 years
34	49.4 years
35	48.5 years
36	47.5 years
37	46.5 years
38	45.6 years
39	44.6 years
40	43.6 years
41	42.7 years
42	41.7 years
43	40.7 years
44	39.8 years
45	38.8 years
46	37.9 years
47	37.0 years
48	36.0 years
49	35.1 years
50	34.2 years

LIFE EXPECTANCY TABLE

Current Age	Life Expectancy (years remaining)
51	33.3 years
52	32.3 years
53	31.4 years
54	30.5 years
55	29.6 years
56	28.7 years
57	27.9 years
58	27.0 years
59	26.1 years
60	25.2 years
61	24.4 years
62	23.5 years
63	22.7 years
64	21.8 years
65	21.0 years
66	20.2 years
67	19.4 years
68	18.6 years
69	17.8 years
70	17.0 years
71	16.3 years
72	15.5 years
73	14.8 years
74	14.1 years
75	13.4 years

LIFE EXPECTANCY TABLE	
Current Age	**Life Expectancy (years remaining)**
76	12.7 years
77	12.1 years
78	11.4 years
79	10.8 years
80	10.2 years
81	9.7 years
82	9.1 years
83	8.6 years
84	8.1 years
85	7.6 years
86	7.1 years
87	6.7 years
88	6.3 years
89	5.9 years
90	5.5 years
91	5.2 years
92	4.9 years
93	4.6 years
94	4.3 years
95	4.1 years
96	3.8 years
97	3.6 years
98	3.4 years
99	3.1 years
100	2.9 years

Bibliography

Benna, Ted and Brenda Watson Newmann, *401(k)s For Dummies*, Wiley Publishing, Indianapolis, 2003.

Hebeler, Henry, *Getting Started in a Financially Secure Retirement: Pre- and Post-Retirement Planning*, John Wiley & Sons, Inc., 2007.

Hetzer, Barbara, *Smart Guide to Maximizing Your 401(k) Plan*, Cader Company, Inc., 1999.

"How to Make A Million At..." series, *Kiplinger's Personal Finance* magazine, February 2008.

Loeper, David, *Stop the 401(k) Rip-off: Eliminate Costly Hidden Fees to Improve Your Life*, Bridgeway Books, 2007.

Malaspina, Margaret A., *Cracking Your Retirement Nest Egg (Without Scrambling Your Finances): 25 Things You Must Know Before You Tap Your 401(k), IRA, or Other Retirement Savings Plan*, Bloomberg Press, 2003.

Rogers, Craig and Dale Rogers, *How to Build, Protect and Maintain Your 401(k) Plan: Strategies and Tactics*, Marketplace Books, 2004.

Slott, Ed, *The Retirement Savings Time Bomb...and How to Defuse It*, 2nd Edition, Penguin Books, 2007.

Spragins, Ellyn, "A Guide to Managing Your 401(k)," *Newsweek*, December 16, 1996.

Updegrave, Walter, "To Roth or not to Roth 401(k)," *Money* magazine, January 17, 2008.

Weinstein, Grace, *Winning With Your 401(k): Creating the Right Portfolio for You*, John Wiley & Sons, Inc., 2001.

 # Author Biography

Heather Kleba is a journalist living in Washington, D.C. She graduated with a Bachelor of Arts in Journalism and a minor in Political Science from The George Washington University. She currently works for *Governing* magazine, a publication covering state and local politics, where she writes about issues including finance, the environment, technology, health care, and management. She also helps plan and coordinate conferences and other events that bring together state and local government officials to discuss solutions to problems in government. In her spare time, Heather enjoys spending time with her fiancé, planning their wedding, and traveling.

Index

C

Cafeteria Plan, 263

CD, 96-97, 208, 263

Certificate of Deposit, 134, 263

CODA, 263

Compensation, 239, 263

Compounding, 34, 157, 171, 201, 243-244, 250, 263

D

Defined Benefit Plans, 27-29, 32, 60, 242, 263

Defined Contribution Plans, 23, 26-29, 32, 43, 242-243, 245, 263

Department of Labor, 276, 38, 69, 77, 89-90, 99, 208, 264-265

Determination Letter, 264

Direct Transfer, 155, 264

Disclosure, 77, 264

Distribution, 30, 161, 165-167, 171, 209, 212, 216, 219, 264, 266-267

Diversification, 34, 53, 101, 103, 105, 111-112, 117-118, 121, 125, 130, 139-141, 144, 147, 187, 202, 245, 7, 11

Dollar-cost Averaging, 106, 245, 264

E

Employee Benefits Security Administration, 77, 90, 265

Employee Retirement Income Security Act, 38, 66, 265

Employee Stock Option Plan, 265

Employee Stock Ownership Plan, 265

ESOP, 265

ESPP, 28, 265

Excess Aggregate Contributions, 265

F

Fidelity Bond, 69, 266

Fiduciary, 38, 66-67, 69, 74, 79-80, 86-88, 90-91, 99, 222, 243, 266, 272

Form 1099R, 266

Form 5500, 77, 229, 266

G

Guaranteed Investment Contracts, 95, 131, 134, 266, 7

I

Insurance, 273, 38, 52, 90, 97, 131, 134-136, 164, 180, 199, 216, 236, 238, 256, 262, 266

IRS, 273, 276-277, 75, 77, 89, 158-160, 166, 180, 208, 213, 221, 231, 264-267, 270

J

Job Force, 101, 139, 148, 166, 181, 193, 196-197, 204, 209, 16, 8

K

Keogh, 230-231, 267, 9

L

Large-cap Stocks, 97, 267

M

Monte Carlo Analysis, 268

Mutual Fund, 274, 64, 93, 98, 117-123, 142, 202, 207-209, 229, 237, 268

N

NASDAQ, 274, 114, 268-269

P

Pension, 276, 27-28, 32, 54, 58, 75, 82, 84-85, 99, 112, 123, 207, 219, 223, 225, 231, 238, 245, 258, 267, 269, 16, 11

Profit sharing plan, 270

Q

Qualified Domestic Relations Order, 68, 270

Qualified Joint and Survivor Annuity, 270

R

S

T

V